Year 5

English Grammar

AGE 9-11

Boswell Taylor

As a parent, you can play a major role in your child's education by your interest and encouragement. This book is designed to give your child an understanding of the rules of English grammar. Confidence in the basic principles of English will help improve your child's work in other school subjects.

The book introduces each part of speech in turn, with exercises to practise each point. There is a test to check your child's understanding before moving on to the next part of speech. Answers for all the exercises and tests can be found at the back of the book. Over the page you will find advice on how to help your child get the most out of this book.

Hodder Children's Books

NATIONAL CONFEDERATION OF PARENT TEACHER ASSOCIATIONS

NCPTA

The only home learning programme supported by the NCPTA

How to help your child

● Make sure your child completes all the exercises for each grammar point. The rules themselves are quite abstract, and the best way to learn them is through plenty of practice.

● If you find your child is getting answers wrong, don't make a big issue out of it. Simply talk through the relevant grammar point to make sure it has been fully understood, then suggest your child has another go at the exercises.

● Always take a positive approach, and concentrate on your child's successes by giving praise and encouragement.

● A good dictionary is an excellent investment which will help your child to make the best use of this book. Your child's teacher or a local bookseller or librarian may be able to recommend one.

Published by Hodder Children's Books 1995

Copyright © Boswell Taylor 1989

The right of Boswell Taylor to be identified as the author of the Work has been asserted by him in accordance with the Copyright, Designs and Patents Act 1988.

Printed and bound in Great Britain

Hodder Children's Books
A division of Hodder Headline
338 Euston Road
London NW1 3BH

Previously published as Test Your Child's English Grammar

Facts about the parts of speech

We speak and write the English language. The structure that provides the word patterns is known as grammar. When we study grammar, we study how words are put together to form sentences. We rarely think about sentences or grammar when we speak and write. The words fall naturally into some sort of pattern. Sometimes the pattern is correct, and sometimes it is not. The use of correct grammar means that the correct meaning is conveyed. Incorrect grammar introduces confusion to the word patterns.

Word patterns are composed of parts of speech. Each part of speech has its own special function. There are eight (some say nine)* separate functions or jobs; there are eight parts of speech. Here they are:

Part of speech	Function	Examples
Noun	naming word	sausage, Jack
Pronoun	substitute for noun	she, he, it, they
Verb	doing word	walk, think
Adjective	describing word	proud, beautiful
Adverb	word modifying action	run *quickly*, work *late*
Preposition	relates one thing to another	ship *on* the sea, jump *over* the wall
Conjunction	joining word	the driver *and* the passenger
Interjection	expresses emotion	Oh! Ouch!

* Sometimes the three 'articles' *a, an* (indefinite) and *the* (definite) are called a part of speech.

Every word in this book and in every book belongs to one of the parts of speech.

Nouns

A noun is the name of a person, animal, place or thing. Everything has a name, such as **chair**, **ship**, **football**. Everybody has a name. There is the common name, such as **person**. **Boy** and **girl** are nouns to tell us the kind of **person**. Then every boy and every girl has a proper name, such as **William** or **Emma**. All the words printed here in bold type are nouns.

Underline each noun in the following sentences:

A 1 I patted a <u>dog</u>, stroked a <u>cat</u>, rode on an <u>elephant</u> and fed a <u>seal</u>.

   2 I sat on a chair, drank from a cup, ate off a plate and used a spoon.

   3 I played in the park, sailed a ship, built a sand-castle and flew a kite.

   4 I played football with William, John, Fred and Craig.

Write the most suitable noun from the list in each empty space:

snake, horse, lion, mouse, sparrow, frog

B 1 The ......*mouse*........ squeaked.   2 The ....neighed.

   3 The .... hissed.   4 The .... croaked.

   5 The .... chirped.   6 The .... roared.

Singular and Plural (Number)

Nouns can have either singular ('one') or plural ('more than one') number. Generally the plural is formed by adding **-s** or **-es** to the singular, but there are exceptions. In the exercise below, all the words are exceptions to the rule. Some words, like sheep, are both singular and plural.

Fill the gaps to complete the chart.

	Singular	*Plural*		*Singular*	*Plural*
C 1	knife	*knives*	2	....	thieves
3	child	....	4	....	geese
5	tooth	....	6	....	sheep

Nouns – Gender

Gender concerns the two sexes, male and female.
Masculine gender denotes the male sex, such as **man**, **father**, **boy**.
Feminine gender denotes the female sex, such as **woman**, **mother**, **girl**.
We also have Neuter gender and Common gender.
Neuter gender denotes things without sex, such as **ball**, **church**.
Common gender denotes either sex, such as **child**, **person**, **teacher**.

Fill the gaps to complete the chart:

	Masculine	Feminine		Masculine	Feminine
A 1	_abbot_	abbess	2	god	....
3	grandfather	....	4	....	nun
5	....	cow	6	gander	....
7	emperor	....	8	....	lady
9	....	princess	10	husband	....
11	nephew	....	12	....	daughter
13	....	ewe	14	stallion	....
15	bridegroom	....	16	....	duchess
17	....	landlady	18	uncle	....
19	son-in-law	....	20	....	heiress

Change all masculines to corresponding feminines in the following:

B 1 The wizard changed the prince to a frog.
   The witch changed the princess to a frog.

   2 The king awarded a medal to the hero.

   ....

   3 The page followed the bridegroom into the church.

   ....

   4 The policeman arrested the murderer.

   ....

   5 The heir to the whole estate was a penniless actor.

   ....

Gender

Common gender words are unisex words. The same word is both male and female.

Neuter gender denotes non-living things that are neither male nor female.

Here are 49 nouns.   *Underline* the 24 words with Common gender.

Cross out the 25 words with Neuter gender.

A <u>child</u>   ~~chair~~   <u>friend</u>   <u>parent</u>   ~~school~~   <u>scholar</u>   <u>pig</u>
   house   mountain deer   volcano   singer   owner   window
   passenger pop-song explorer swimmer   ladder   radio   sheep
   fowl   boots   librarian desk   book   bird   ice-cream
   people   road   animal   sausage   onlookers balloon   choir
   rain   dagger   journalist mob   thunder   reader   coal
   car   canal   monarch   canoe   fish   door   lemonade

Families

A sheep can be a ewe (female), a ram (male) or a lamb (young animal). These are the names (nouns) of the members of nine families all jumbled up:

lion, bitch, foal, bull, mare, piglet, sow, stallion, duckling, drake, cock, goose, cub, cow, buck, lioness, gosling, puppy, dog, gander, boar, calf, duck, chick, fawn, hen, doe

Use names from the list above to complete the chart to make happy families.

	Male	Female	Young animal
B 1	lion	lioness	cub
2	gander		
3			piglet
4		bitch	
5	drake		
6		mare	
7			fawn
8	bull		
9		hen	

Group Terms or Collective Nouns

A collective noun names a group of individuals as if they were one individual:

committee (of people)   **herd** (of cattle)   **pack** (of cards)

They may be singular or plural:

one team of players   two teams of players
The committee is made up of boys and girls.
The committee are quarrelling among themselves again.

Special group terms are used with both animate (living) and inanimate (non-living) things.
These are collective nouns:

crew, choir, flock, gang, company, swarm, litter, stud, shoal, school

Fill the gaps with the correct collective noun.

Animate (living things)

A 1 ....*litter*........... of puppies   2 ....of sailors

3 .... of birds   4 .... of actors

5 .... of thieves   6 .... of whales

7 .... of herring   8 .... of singers

9 .... of horses   10 .... of bees

These are collective nouns:

library, suit, crate, fleet, bunch, bouquet, string, chest, bundle, set

Fill the gaps with the correct collective noun.

Inanimate (non-living things)

B 1 ...*bouquet*......... of flowers   2 ....of books

3 .... of beads   4 .... of clothes

5 .... of grapes   6 .... of drawers

7 .... of tools   8 .... of ships

9 .... of rags   10 .... of fruit

★ Now test yourself in the use of nouns

Write the singular of the following:

A   1   children   2   geese   3   boxes ....

     4   men   5   passers-by   6   teeth ....

Write the plural of the following:

B   1   woman   2   sheep   3   loaf ....

     4   echo   5   mouse-trap   6   foot ....

Write the masculine equivalent of the following:

C   1   goddess   2   wife   3   bride ....

     4   empress................   5   niece   6   female ....

Write the feminine equivalent of the following:

D   1   lion   2   uncle   3   wizard ....

     4   traitor   5   monk   6   headmaster ....

Complete the chart to make happy families:

	Male	Female	Young	Male	Female	Young
E	1 leopard	....	2	sow		....
	3 ram	....	4	....	calf	

Fill the gaps with the correct collective nouns.

F   1   .... of soldiers   2   ....of cattle

    3   .... of sheep   4   .... of wolves

    5   .... of lions   6   .... of geese

    7   .... of mackerel   8   .... of furniture

Write the most appropriate word for a number of people:

G   1   at a music concert   2   in church ....

     3   in a bus   4   in a supermarket ....

Write one word for a number of things:

H   1   .... of bananas   2   .... of bells

     3   .... of strawberries   4   .... of islands

Pronouns

Pronouns are used in place of nouns. Look at these sentences:

Peter caught **the ball**. **Peter** bounced **the ball**. **Peter** kicked **the ball** upfield.

There is too much repetition. We can use 'he' instead of 'Peter' and 'it' instead of 'ball', like this:

Peter caught **the ball**. **He** bounced **it**. **He** kicked **it** upfield.

We cannot change the name 'Peter' to 'he' in the first sentence, or 'ball' to 'it' or we would not know to whom 'he' referred and to what 'it' referred. A pronoun must always have a noun nearby to which it refers.

There are seven personal pronouns. They are the 'doers':

I   you   he   she   it   we   they

Each one makes sense if it is used to complete this sentence: ....saw Louise.

I saw Louise.   **You** saw Louise.   **He** saw Louise.   **She** saw Louise.
It saw Louise.   **We** saw Louise.   **They** saw Louise.

Each of these 'doers' has a 'receiver'. Something happens to it.

me   you   him   her   it   us   them

Each one makes sense if it is used to complete this sentence:
Louise saw ....

In each of the following you are given the 'doer' (the subjective). Put the correct 'receiver' (the objective) in the gap.

A 1 I saw Louise. Louise saw ...*me*....   2 You saw Louise. Louise saw ....

   3 He saw Louise. Louise saw ....   4 She saw Louise. Louise saw ....

   5 It saw Louise. Louise saw ....   6 We saw Louise. Louise saw ....

   7 They saw Louise. Louise saw ....

Write these sentences. Use pronouns instead of the nouns shown in *italics*.

B 1 Duncan went to the circus. *Duncan* went with his friends.
      Duncan went to the circus. He went with his friends.

   2 Yasmin plays tennis. *Yasmin* is good at the game.

      ....

   3 The snake saw the bird. *The snake* glided away.

Each of the personal pronouns has a possessive pronoun. These are the 'owners':

Nominative ('doers'):	I	you	he	she	it	we	you	they
Objective ('receivers'):	me	you	him	her	it	us	you	them
Possessive ('owners'):	mine	yours	his	hers	its	ours	yours	theirs

Complete the following, adding the correct possessive pronouns:

A 1 I bought the bike. It is my bike. The bike is ....

  2 You bought the bike. It is your bike. The bike is ....

  3 He bought the bike. It is his bike. The bike is ....

  4 She bought the bike. It is her bike. The bike is ....

  5 The dog caught the ball. It is his ball. The ball is ....

  6 We bought the books. They are our books. The books are ....

  7 They bought the books. They are their books. The books are ....

We can add **'self'** or **'selves'** to a personal pronoun to make a compound pronoun. Such compound pronouns are called reflexive pronouns because they look back on themselves.

  myself yourself himself herself itself ourselves themselves

Complete the following, adding the correct reflexive pronoun:

B   1 I feed ...*myself*..........   2 You feed ....   3 He feeds ....

  4 She feeds .... 5 It feeds .... 6 We feed ....

  7 They feed ....

Three pronouns are used to ask questions. They are called interrogative (questioning) pronouns. They are: **Who? Which? What?**
Complete the following, adding the correct interrogative pronouns:

C 1 ...*Who*.......... are you? I am Moira.

  2 .... class are you in? I am in Class Two.

  3 .... is your name? My name is Moira O'Farrell.

These pronouns (called definite pronouns) answer the question 'Which?':
  this these that those

Complete the following, adding the correct definite pronouns:

D 1 Which cake is yours? ...*This*..... is my cake, ... cake is his.

  2 Which buns are yours? .... are our buns, ... buns are theirs.

★ Now test yourself in the use of pronouns

In the following there are groups of two words in the brackets. One of the words is correct, and the other is wrong. Cross out the wrong word.

A   1 (I, Me) listened to pop-music with (she, her).
     2 Her brother is taller than (we, us) are, but she is smaller than
       (I, me) am.
     3 Between you and (I, me) no one knows the secret.
     4 It is (they, them) we want to join the club.
     5 I know your face. (Who, What) is your name?
     6 (Who, Which) is writing his name in the book?
     7 The teacher knows (we, us) are sometimes annoyed with (us, ourselves).
     8 Was it (I, me) you saw at the party with (they, them)?
     9 (This, That) is your book here, and (this, that) is my book over there.
    10 Laura caught Becky and (she, her), but she did not catch Ann
       and (I, me).
    11 Nicholas is cleverer than (he, him) is, but not as clever as (I, me) am.
    12 This is the man (who, which) frightened (we, us).
    13 I played all day with (he, him) and (she, her).
    14 It curled (himself, itself) up and went to sleep.
    15 Those are (they, them).

From the evidence given at the trial of the Knave of Hearts in *Alice in Wonderland* by Lewis Carroll:

     1 They told me you had been to her,

     2 And mentioned me to him:

     3 She gave me a good character,

     4 But said I could not swim.

     5 He sent them word I had not gone,

     6 (We know it to be true:)

     7 If she should push the matter on,

     8 What would become of you?

B   Underline the 16 pronouns in the above verse.

C   Why is the passage so difficult to understand?

....

....

Adjectives

An adjective is a word that adds to the meaning of a noun. It is sometimes called a 'describing' word. These words are descriptive adjectives:

fat   soft   beautiful   cruel   hard-hearted   charming

Underline the descriptive adjectives in the following:

A 1 The <u>beautiful</u> princess helped the <u>frail old</u> man to rise.
  2 The cruel wolves tracked the wounded beast across the deep snow.
  3 Into the icy water the brave woman dived again and again.
  4 When the heavy lid was raised the brilliant jewels could be seen.
  5 The limping footballer scored the winning goal.

These are adjectives of quantity:
  Definite quantities: all the numerals (**one, two, three** and so on)
                        second, third, fourth and so on
                        both, double, treble and so on
  Indefinite quantities: **few, some, many, all, several, any**

Underline the adjectives of quantity in the following:

B 1 <u>Several</u> children took part in <u>both</u> plays.
  2 Some rain fell on the third day of the holidays.
  3 A few fish lurked under the second bridge.
  4 Many children had double helpings of chips.
  5 All pupils are expected to bring some toys to the fair.

Some adjectives put a limit on the noun.
Demonstrative adjectives **this   that   these   those**
  point out the object being talked or written about.
Interrogative adjectives **which   whose   what**
  ask questions about some object or person.
Distributive adjectives **each   every   either   neither   a   an   the**
  refer to individual objects or people.

Underline the limiting adjectives in the following:

C 1 <u>This</u> trophy belongs to <u>every</u> pupil.
  2 Neither child lives in that street.
  3 Which picture do you like best?
  4 Whose photograph hangs on the wall?
  5 The perfume costs a pound a fluid ounce.

Adjectives – degrees of comparison

The positive degree is the simple form of the adjective. It is the form shown in a dictionary entry: **cold beautiful callous swift great**

The comparative degree is used to compare two persons or two things:

Almost all adjectives of one syllable and many adjectives of two syllables form the comparative by adding **-r** or **-er** to the simple adjective.

cold becomes **colder**   **swift** becomes **swifter**   **great** becomes **greater**

Write the comparative form by the side of the simple adjective:

A   1 brave ....*braver*....   2 quick ....   3 fine ....

4 short ....   5 large ....   6 small ....

7 narrow ....   8 pleasant ....   9 shallow ....

Some adjectives of two syllables also add **-r** or **-er**, but spelling rules mean that changes have to be made to the simple adjectives:

ugly becomes **uglier**   **thin** becomes **thinner**

Many adjectives of two syllables or more form the comparative by using **more** before the simple adjective:

careless becomes **more careless**   **beautiful** becomes **more beautiful**

The superlative degree is used in comparing three or more persons or things.

Almost all adjectives of one syllable and many of two syllables form the superlative by adding **-st** or **-est** to the simple adjective:

cold becomes **coldest swift** becomes **swiftest great** becomes **greatest**

Write by the side of the simple adjective the superlative form:

B   1 brave ...*bravest*.....   2 quick ....   3 fine ....

4 short ....   5 large ....   6 small ....

7 narrow ....   8 pleasant ....   9 shallow ....

Many adjectives of two syllables or more form the superlative by using **most** before the simple adjective:

Careless becomes **most careless**   **beautiful** becomes **most beautiful**

★ Now test yourself in the use of adjectives

Underline the adjectives in the following sentences:

A   1   The skilful driver kept his racing car steady on the slippery road.
2   The kind lady dropped a small coin into the collecting box.
3   The careless climber slipped from the narrow crumbling path.
4   The fierce little creature attacked the terrified bird.
5   Three boys and two girls ate several cakes each.
6   Any pupil in the fourth year would envy those lucky boys.
7   Some people with cold hands are supposed to have warm hearts.
8   The thief – cold-blooded, cruel and greedy – killed the little dog.
9   Each girl took every advantage of the holiday.
10   Those earrings should not be worn at school.
11   Whose work is this excellent picture?
12   Which skates belong to neither girl?

Complete the following chart.

		Positive	Comparative	Superlative
B	1	mild	milder	mildest
	2	beautiful	....	....
	3	rich	....	....
	4	simple	....	....
	5	benevolent	....	....
	6	fierce	....	....

Complete this chart which consists of adjectives compared irregularly.

C	1	little	less	least
	2	many, much	....	....
	3	bad	....	....
	4	good	....	....
	5	far (for information)	....	....
	6	far (distance)	....	....

Verbs

The verb is an important part of the sentence. Nearly all sentences contain a verb.

A verb may express action, such as **swim, run, sing, fall, throw.**
It is therefore sometimes called the 'doing' word.

Underline the verb in the following.

A   1   Joanne <u>reads</u> the book.

2   The boy danced on to the stage.

3   The horse neighed.

4   The tortoise crawled slowly across the stony path.

5   With a splash the bucket dropped into the well.

6   Stand to attention for the officer.

7   Before the end of the concert the choir sang two ballads.

8   The lightning flashed and the thunder clashed.

9   The lion quietly stalks its prey.

10   My mother wrote to the manager.

A verb may express a state of being, such as **is, are, am**. Other linking words that express a state or condition are **feel** (ill), **look** (smart), **taste** (sweet).

Underline the verb in the following:

B   1   The children <u>are</u> on the field.

2   I am ready.

3   The dog is in his kennel.

4   The beaten team seems happy enough despite their defeat.

5   The dogs are wild in the garden.

6   The teacher sounds angry and the class grows quiet.

7   Remain still until you are ready.

8   The household guards look smart in their uniform.

9   The battle seems lost.

10   The umpire appears satisfied.

Auxiliary verbs

Sometimes we use two words to complete the verb. The lesser verbs that help the main verb are known as auxiliary verbs. Auxiliary verbs are: **is, are, was, were, may, might, should, would, will, shall, can, could, do, did, had, have, has.**

Underline the *two words* that complete the verb in the following:

A 1 The woman <u>has</u> <u>tried</u>.
  2 The ship will arrive.
  3 The boy might copy his neighbour's work.
  4 I shall run all the way to the station.
  5 The aircraft should land soon.
  6 The old man was injured in the road-accident.

The auxiliary verb may be separated from the main verb by another word or words.

The baby had never walked before.
The driver can very rarely take passengers.

Sometimes we need three words to complete a verb.

The wheel should be changed before Saturday.
The pirate has been wounded by the sailor.

Underline the verbs in the following:

B 1 The car <u>will</u> <u>be</u> <u>bought</u>.
  2 You should have waited for your little brother.
  3 The whistle had been blown before the goal was scored.
  4 The pony jumped the wall.
  5 The painting will be finished by morning.
  6 The painter had nearly finished her work.
  7 When the clock strikes nine the work will be done.
  8 The jockey whipped his horse.
  9 The lorry will go faster down the hill.
  10 Come along!
  11 You may want a new bike but you will never get it.
  12 Stand and deliver!

Number in the Verb – singular or plural

If the subject is singular (only one) the verb is singular.
If the subject is plural (more than one) the verb is plural.

> *Singular* (one only): I **walk**, you **walk**, he **walks**, she **walks**, it **walks**.
> *Plural* (more than one): we **walk**, you **walk**, they **walk**.

Complete the following using the correct number in the verb:

A 1   I play, he ..*plays*.., she ...*plays*.., it ..*plays*.., you ..*play*.., we ..*play*....

   2   I run, he runs, she ...., it ...., we ...., they ....

   3   I jump, he ...., she ...., it ...., we ...., they ....

   4   I fall, she ...., it ...., you ...., we ...., they ....

   5   I hit, he ...., she ...., you ...., they ...., we ....

   6   I ...., he writes, she ...., it ...., you ...., they ....

Note final **-es** *(spelling rule)*

   7   I catch, he catches, she ...., it ...., you ...., we ....

   8   I wish, he ...., she ...., you ...., we ...., they ....

Note change of final **-y** *to* **-ies** *in the third person singular (spelling rule)*

   9   I try, he tries, she ...., you ...., it ...., we ...., they ....

 10   I cry, he ...., she ...., you ...., we ...., they ....

Tenses in the Verb – present and past

The tense of a verb shows when an action takes place.
Present tense shows that an action takes place now or is completed now.

> she **walks**   she **is walk*ing***   she **has walked**   she **has been walk*ing***

Note the words ending in *-ing*. They are known as present participles
They show continuous action.
Past tense shows that an action took place yesterday or at some previous time.

> she **walk*ed*** she **was walking** she **had walk*ed*** she **had been walking**

The simple past tense in regular verbs is formed by adding **-ed.**
The past participle, which ends in **-ed** or can be irregular (see page 18), shows completed action.

Principal parts of irregular verbs that cause trouble

Present	Past	Past participle	Present	Past	Past participle
am, be	was	been	give	gave	given
awake	awaked	awakened	go	went	gone
	awoke		grow	grew	grown
bear	bore	borne	hear	heard	heard
begin	began	begun	hide	hid	hidden
bend	bent	bent	kneel	knelt	knelt
bite	bit	bitten	know	knew	known
blow	blew	blown	lay	laid	laid
break	broke	broken	leave	left	left
bring	brought	brought	lose	lost	lost
catch	caught	caught	make	made	made
choose	chose	chosen	pay	paid	paid
come	came	come	ride	rode	ridden
do	did	done	ring	rang	rung
draw	drew	drawn	run	ran	run
drink	drank	drunk	say	said	said
eat	ate	eaten	sell	sold	sold
fall	fell	fallen	shake	shook	shaken
feel	felt	felt	sing	sang	sung
fly	flew	flown	swim	swam	swum
forget	forgot	forgotten	tear	tore	torn
freeze	froze	frozen	write	wrote	written
get	got	got			

Using the auxiliary verbs

Except for the simple present and the simple past tenses all tenses are formed with the auxiliary verbs **do, have, had, be, shall, will, should** and **would**. In speech, auxiliaries are often contracted (shortened).

> **is** and **has** become **'s**   **He's** working   **She's** gone home.
> **had** and **would** become **'d**   **He'd** scored. **She'd** often go to the pictures.

The negative is usually formed by adding not before the main verb.

I shall **not** go.   She was **not** playing.

In a dictionary, verbs are usually shown in their infinitive form:

(to) **catch**, (to) **shop**, (to) **fly**, (to) **learn**, (to) **forget**, (to) **hit**, (to) **mark,** (to) **climb**

★ Now test yourself in the use of verbs

Underline the verbs in the following sentences:

A 1 The detective arrested the thief.

   2 In the murky water the diver fought the octopus.

   3 Kick the ball into the goal.

   4 The farmer ploughed the field in autumn.

B 1 They had caught the lost dog.

   2 I will telephone you in the morning.

   3 The most daring of the children would climb the tree.

   4 The team will be pleased with the result.

C 1 Once more the king is on the throne.

   2 The apple tastes sweet and the orange tastes bitter.

   3 If you feel ill tomorrow you will stay in bed.

   4 Now you are here I should really like you to stay.

Write the past tense of the following (you can use the chart on page 18):

D 1 bring .... 2 swim .... 3 kneel ....

   4 blow .... 5 say .... 6 lose ....

Write the past participle of the following:

E 1 draw .... 2 sell .... 3 lay ....

   4 break .... 5 fly .... 6 write ....

Fill each gap correctly with one of these words: know, known, knew, knows.

F 1 I .... the answer now.

   2 I .... yesterday that you were not well.

   3 I have .... the dog all my life.

   4 He .... his way to the market, and goes there every week.

   5 I will .... what to do when I see him tomorrow.

   6 I would like to .... her very much.

Adverbs

An adverb is a word that modifies or adds to the meaning of another word: a verb, an adjective or another verb.
Most adverbs are derived from adjectives by the addition of **-ly**.

> **slow** becomes **slowly**   **bad** becomes **badly**

Write the equivalent adverb for the following adverbs:

Adjective	Adverb	Adjective	Adverb
A 1 quick	...*quickly*....	2 neat	....
3 loud	....	4 clear	....
5 free	....	6 brave	....

Sometimes the adverb is changed in spelling (see spelling rules).

Write the equivalent adjective for the following adverbs:

Adjective	Adverb	Adjective	Adverb
B 1 ..*greedy*....	greedily	2	easily
3	humbly	4	gently

Some adverbs do not end in -ly. They have the same form as adjectives.
Complete each sentence with the correct adverb:

Adjective	Sentence with adverb
C 1 a *hard* job	I worked ......*hard*.......... to get the job finished.
2 an *early* train	The train arrived .... at the station.
3 a *fast* race	The girls ran .... to get there first.
4 a *short* stick	The wind made the ball fall .... of the goal.

Adverbs tell **how**, **when**, **where**, and **how much**.
Adverbs of manner answer the question **How?**
e.g. **badly**, **easily**, **slowly**, **well**, **surely**, **loudly**, **quietly**, **clumsily**

D 1 The children played ..*quietly*..... so that they should not disturb the sleeping man.

2 Debbie fell .... off her bike and sprained her ankle.

3 The knight shouted .... to make himself heard.

4 The tortoise crawled .... but still won the race.

Adverbs of time answer the question **When?**

e.g. **today, soon, yesterday, before, now, since, seldom, often, immediately, already**

Complete each sentence with one of the adverbs listed above:

A 1 He came ..... *yesterday* .... and stayed the night.

2 Start .... the whistle is blown.

3 We have swimming .... and games tomorrow.

4 Comets .... appear in the sky.

5 The horse has .... won two races before this one.

6 I will run and .... catch him up.

Adverbs of place answer the question **Where?**

e.g. **here, everywhere, above, behind, outside, west, in, out, straight, nowhere**

Complete each sentence with one of the adverbs listed above:

B 1 He searched .. *everywhere* ..... but could not find the treasure.

2 The wind blows .... but the hut is snug inside.

3 The arrow went .... to its target.

4 The bridesmaids followed close .... the bride.

5 He went in dry and came .... wet.

6 The church spire could be seen high .... the trees.

Adverbs of degree answer the question **How much?**

e.g. **almost, completely, less, thoroughly, quite, very, too, hardly, entirely, so**

Complete each sentence with one of the adverbs listed above:

C 1 The tired old man walked .... *very* .... slowly.

2 I have .... finished mowing the lawn and then I will rest.

3 When the boys are .... ready we will go.

4 I have .... money now I have finished shopping.

5 Dry your hair .... or you will catch cold.

6 Your work is .... good I am giving you full marks.

Interrogative adverbs are **When? Where? Why?** Relative adverbs are **when, where, why.**

Adverbs – degrees of comparison

Adverbs are compared in the same way as adjectives (see page 13).
The positive degree is the simplest form of the adverb. It is the form shown in a dictionary entry: **bravely   slowly   early   badly   much**

The comparative degree is used to compare two persons or things.
The superlative degree is used to compare three or more persons or things.

Adverbs of one syllable usually form the comparative degree by adding **-er** and the superlative degree by adding **-est**

Compare this chart:

	Positive	Comparative	Superlative
A 1	soon	sooner	soonest
2	hard		
3	fast		
4	late		
5	early		

Adverbs of two syllables or more generally form the comparative by adding **more** and the superlative by adding **most**

Compare this chart:

	Positive	Comparative	Superlative
B 1	briefly	more briefly	most briefly
2	happily		
3	quickly		
4	carefully		
5	easily		

Complete this chart of exceptions:

	Positive	Comparative	Superlative
C 1	badly, ill	worse	worst
2	far		
3	little		
4	much, many		
5	well		

★ Now test yourself in the use of adverbs

Underline the adverbs in the following:

A   1 The footballers will soon be ready and the match can begin.

   2 The girl formerly lived with her grandmother.

   3 The fox withdrew quickly into the wood.

   4 The children behaved badly at the circus.

   5 Jennifer once heard a mouse in the cupboard.

   6 Where was the escaped prisoner hiding?

Complete the following with the adverbs from this list: **gleefully, impudently, smartly, bitterly, greedily, lovingly, fitfully, tunefully**

B   1 The cheeky girl answered ....   2 The sentry saluted ....

   3 He chuckled ....   4 The hungry boy ate ....

   5 The cat was caressed ....   6 The choir sang ....

   7 The dog slept ....   8 The wind blew ....

Complete the following chart:

Positive	Comparative	Superlative
C 1 willingly	....	....
2 ill	....	....
3 early	....	....
4 loudly	....	....
5 seriously	....	....
6 fearfully	....	....

Complete the following with the correct comparatives and superlatives of these adverbs: **closely, quickly, late, brightly, hard, carefully.**

D   1 You walked quickly but John walked ....

   2 We both moved carefully, but I moved .... than you.

   3 The lights shone brightly, but the stage lights shone ....

   4 He looked at the insect closely, and then he looked .... still.

   5 I tried hard, but Jill tried even ....

   6 I came late, but Jamila was the .... to arrive.

Conjunctions

Conjunctions join together words or word groups.

Here are five simple conjunctions that are used to join together groups of words of equal value: **and   but   nor   or   yet**

Complete each of the following with the most suitable conjunction from the list above:

A 1 Katie ....*and*........ Maggie are friends.

2 He was a giant, ... he was weak.

3 The book was not on the shelves, ... was it on the desk.

4 I will smile if I win .... if we lose.

5 We quarrel .... we are friends.

Some conjunctions are used in pairs: **both ... and, so ... as, either ... or, neither ... nor, whether ... or**

Complete each of the following with the most suitable conjunction from the pairs listed above:

B 1 <u>Both</u> the highwayman ....*and*...... the innkeeper were guilty.

2 The goal was missed by .... the striker and the winger.

3 Would you be so good .... to repeat the directions?

4 Either you will confess .... I will tell the whole story.

5 .... Freddie nor Lynn wants to go to the party.

6 It does not matter to me whether you play .... not.

Underline both conjunctions in each sentence above.

Conjunctions can be grouped according to their special meanings.
They can express *Time, Place, Reason, Concession, Condition, Manner, Purpose, Result.*

Time **when while as since till until after before whenever**
Place **where wherever**
Reason **because since as**
Concession **although though while as even if whether ... or**
Condition **if unless**

24

Manner **as**   **as if**   **as ... as**   **so ... as**   **than**   **as though**
Purpose **so that**
Result **so ... that**

Complete the following sentences to make sense.
Underline the conjunctions.

A 1 <u>When</u> the pie was opened, the birds ....*began to sing*............

   2 You must wash your hands before ....

   3 After you have eaten your supper ....

   4 I have not spoken to her since ....

   5 .... until you come.

   6 .... while the cat was asleep.

   7 As the dog barked ....

   8 I shall not see him till ....

B 1 He found the ball where ....

   2 Wherever the old man went ....

   3 I shall not come to the party because ....

   4 .... since you cannot hear.

   5 As it is Bonfire Night ....

C 1 I will not go to town even if ....

   2 Although she asked the pianist to play ....

   3 You will take part whether .... or not.

   4 Victoria will not swim in the pool unless ....

   5 If the shop is open ....

   6 I opened the gate into the field so that ....

   7 She acted her part as if ....

   8 As quick as lightning ....

Prepositions

Most prepositions are short words (**to, on, for**). Some prepositions are longer words (**underneath, alongside**). Some prepositions are even groups of words (**as far as, in spite of**).
Prepositions are normally placed before nouns or pronouns. They show the relation of one word (usually a noun or a pronoun) to some other word in the sentence.

The cat is **on** the mat. (**on** shows the position of the cat)
The cat walked **towards** its basket. (**towards** shows direction)
The cat goes out **after** dark. (**after** shows the time when the cat goes out)

The most common prepositions are:

up   down   in   on   at   with   of   for   over   by   between   towards   to

Complete the following adding the most suitable preposition from the list above.

A 1 We arrived ....*on*............ Monday.

2 The girl curtseyed and gave the bouquet .... the queen.

3 The ship sailed .... the desert island.

4 The firemen slid .... the poles.

5 The horse leapt .... the gate.

6 Danny placed the cheese .... the two slices of bread.

7 The mountaineer climbed .... the vertical cliff.

8 The children swam .... the sea every day.

9 The mermaid looked .... her reflection in the water.

Write three suitable and different prepositions for each sentence.

B 1 The book lay ....*in*.............. the box.

2 The book lay .... the box.

3 The book lay .... the box.

4 The skier raced .... the flags.

5 The skier raced .... the flags.

6 The skier raced .... the flags.

More prepositions

The following list consists of common prepositions:

about   after   from   to   within

Complete the following adding the most suitable preposition from each list:

A 1 The tortoise tucked its head ...._within_........ the shell.

  2 The boxer struck his opponent .... the bell sounded.

  3 The park is open .... dawn .... dusk.

  4 The mice ran .... the granary floor.

round   until   into   under   past

B 1 Gather ...._round_.......... and listen to my story.

  2 Go .... the wood .... you come to the blasted oak.

  3 It is now .... bedtime.

  4 You will find the house key .... the mat.

above   near   till   below   off

C 1 The stain can be seen ...._above_.... the window but ...._below_........ the roof.

  2 We will not go home .... morning.

  3 The tiger is now .... the hunters.

  4 I switched .... the light and sat in the dark.

These are prepositions formed from groups of words:

**because of   due to   except for   away from
on top of   in front of   by means of   out of**

Complete the following from the list above:

D 1 I shall not come ...._because of_...... my mother's illness.

  2 All the children played .... Sam and Charles.

  3 This is the money .... you for meals.

  4 Do not stand .... the camera.

  5 Get .... the kicking horse or you will be hurt.

  6 The flag flew .... the church spire.

  7 I saw her when she came .... the shadows.

  8 They entered the castle .... the secret passage.

Interjections

The interjection is a word of exclamation that expresses emotion or feeling. It is sometimes shown by itself followed by an exclamation mark.

Oh! Ugh! Nonsense! Hooray! Ah! Ouch! Ooh! Oh dear! Help! Phew! Oops!

Complete the following adding the most suitable interjection from the list above:

A 1 ....*nonsense!*........... That was a silly remark to make.

 2 .... We have reached our destination at last.

 3 .... I'm very, very hot!

 4 .... You did surprise me.

 5 .... I am drowning!

The interjection is sometimes included in a sentence. It begins the sentence, and the exclamation mark comes at the end of the sentence. The interjection is followed by a comma, and the sentence explains the emotion – the reason for the exclamation.

Complete the following adding the most suitable interjection from the list at the top of the page:

B 1 ....*Ah!*..........., I can see you!

 2 ...., you kicked me!

 3 ...., I've dropped it!

 4 ...., what beautiful chocolates!

 5 ...., I think we're lost!

Articles

the is the definite article and is used for a particular thing.
a (before consonants) and **an** (before a vowel) are indefinite articles.

Complete this sentence:

C The clown climbed .... pole eating .... apple and .... banana.

★ Now test yourself in conjunctions, prepositions and interjections

Complete the following with the most suitable conjunction:

A   1   The horse galloped across the field .... jumped the gate.

     2   The chairman spoke .... he closed the meeting.

     3   You will wait here .... the order is given to go.

     4   Post the notice .... everyone will be able to see it.

     5   We must run .... we are late.

     6   .... I have told her many times she still climbs the tree.

     7   You must go .... you are invited or not.

     8   Let me know .... you want to play.

     9   The opossum can act .... it were dead.

   10   The speaker shouted .... everyone in the vast crowd could hear.

Complete the following with the most suitable preposition:

A   1   The sailor swam .... the drowning man.

     2   The boys climbed .... the greasy pole.

     3   The tired old man leaned .... the wall.

     4   The osprey dived .... the river and caught a fish.

     5   The cashier placed the bags of money .... the counter.

     6   The clown walked .... the tightrope.

     7   The treasure was hidden .... the rubble.

     8   The motor cyclist rode .... the wall of fire.

     9   The paper was wrapped .... the parcel.

   10   The dog jumped .... the fence and escaped.

Complete the following with the most suitable interjection:

C   1   ...., what a shock you gave me.

     2   .... ! It is hot near the fire.

     3   .... , that hurt!

     4   .... ! I have forgotten to bring my money.

     5   .... , we've won!

★ End-of-book test

Read this story:

A *little girl* was painting *industriously* a *picture* of her *favourite meal*. She *carefully painted* a *delicious plate* of *rich crisp chips, baked beans*, white and yellow *fried eggs* and *sizzling fat sausages*. The *teacher* said that she *could show* the picture to the *class* when she *had finished* it.

   The girl painted until the picture *was finished*. Then she *proudly showed* the picture to the class. The class *gasped*, "Oh!" All the painting *was covered* with *red paint*.

   "What a *terrible* thing *to do*!" said the teacher *angrily*. "Who *did* it?"

   "I did," *said* the little girl. "It's *tomato sauce*. I always *have* lots of tomato sauce. I *love* it."

Write twelve nouns from the words in italics in the story above:

A 1 .... 2 .... 3 .... 4 ....

  5 .... 6 .... 7 .... 8 ....

  9 .... 10 .... 11 .... 12 ....

Write twelve verbs (some have more than one word) from the words in *italics* in the story:

B 1 .... 2 .... 3 .... 4 ....

  5 .... 6 .... 7 .... 8 ....

  9 .... 10 .... 11 .... 12 ....

Write twelve adjectives from the words in *italics* in the story above:

C 1 .... 2 .... 3 .... 4 ....

  5 .... 6 .... 7 .... 8 ....

  9 .... 10 .... 11 .... 12 ....

Write four adverbs from the words in *italics* in the story above:

D 1 .... 2 .... 3 .... 4 ....

Answers

Page 4

A   2. chair, cup, plate, spoon   3. park, ship, sand-castle, kite   4. William, John, Fred, Craig

B   2. horse   3. snake   4. frog   5. sparrow   6. lion

C   2. thief   3. children   4. goose   5. teeth   6. sheep

Page 5

A   2. goddess   3. grandmother   4. monk   5. bull   6. goose   7. empress   8. lord/gentleman   9. prince   10. wife
11. niece   12. son   13. ram   14. mare   15. bride   16. duke   17. landlord   18. aunt   19. daughter-in-law   20. heir

B   2. The queen awarded a medal to the heroine.   3. The bridesmaid followed the bride into the church.
4. The policewoman arrested the murderess.   5. The heiress to the whole estate was a penniless actress.

Page 6

A   Common gender: deer, singer, owner, passenger, explorer, swimmer, sheep, fowl, librarian, bird, people, animal,
onlookers, choir, journalist, mob, reader, monarch, fish.
Neuter gender: house, mountain, volcano, window, pop-song, ladder, radio, boots, desk, book, ice-cream, road, sausage,
balloon, rain, dagger, thunder, coal, car, canal, canoe, door, lemonade.

B   2. goose, gosling   3. pig, sow   4. dog, puppy   5. duck, duckling   6. stallion, foal   7. buck, doe   8. cow, calf   9. cock, chick

Page 7

A   2. crew   3. flock   4. company   5. gang   6. school   7. shoal   8. choir   9. stud   10. swarm

B   2. library   3. string   4. suit   5. bunch   6. chest   7. set   8. fleet   9. bundle   10. crate

Page 8. Now test yourself.

A   1. child   2. goose   3. box   4. man   5. passer-by   6. tooth

B   1. women   2. sheep   3. loaves   4. echoes   5. mouse-traps   6. feet

C   1. god   2. husband   3. bridegroom   4. emperor   5. nephew   6. male

D   1. lioness   2. aunt   3. witch   4. traitress   5. nun   6. headmistress

E   1. leopardess, cub   2. boar, piglet   3. ewe, lamb   4. bull, cow

F   1. army   2. herd   3. flock   4. pack   5. pride   6. gaggle   7. shoal   8. suite

G   1. audience   2. congregation   3. passengers   4. customers

H   1. hand   2. peal or ring   3. punnet   4. group

Page 9.

A   2. You   3. him   4. her   5. it   6. us   7. them

B   2. Yasmin plays tennis. She is good at the game.   3. The snake saw the bird. It glided away.

Page 10.

A   1. mine   2. yours   3. his   4. hers   5. his   6. ours   7. theirs

B   2. yourself   3. himself   4. herself   5. itself   6. ourselves   7. themselves

C   2. which   3. what

D   1. that   2. These, those

Page 11.

A   1. I, her   2. we, I   3. me   4. they   5. what   6. who   7. we, ourselves   8. me, them   9. this, that   10. her, me   11. he, I
12. who, us   13. him, her   14. itself   15. they

B   1. they, me, you, her   2. me, him   3. she, me   4. I   5. he, them, I   6. we, it   7. she   8. you

C   We do not know to what or to whom the pronouns apply.

Page 12.

A   2. cruel, wounded, deep   3. icy, brave   4. heavy, brilliant   5. limping, winning

B   2. some, third   3. few, second   4. many, double   5. All, some

C   2. Neither, that   3. Which   4. Whose   5. a

Page 13.

A   2. quicker   3. finer   4. shorter   5. larger   6. smaller   7. narrower   8. pleasanter   9. shallower

B   2. quickest   3. finest   4. shortest   5. largest   6. smallest   7. narrowest   8. pleasantest   9. shallowest

Page 14. Now test yourself.

A   1. skilful, racing, slippery   2. kind, small, collecting   3. careless, narrow, crumbling   4. fierce, little, terrified   5. three,
two, several   6. any, fourth, those, lucky   7. some, cold, warm   8. cold-blooded, cruel, greedy, little   9. each, every
10. those, this   11. whose, excellent   12. which, neither.

B   2. more, most   3. richer, richest   4. simpler, simplest   5. more, most   6. fiercer, fiercest

C   2. more, most   3. worse, worst   4. better, best   5. further, furthest   6. farther, farthest

Page 15

A   2. danced   3. neighed   4. crawled   5. dropped   6. stand   7. sang   8. flashed, clashed   9. stalks   10. wrote

B   2. am   3. is   4. seems   5. are   6. sounds, grows   7. Remain, are   8. look   9. seems   10. appears

Page 16.

A   2. will arrive   3. might copy   4. shall run   5. should land   6. was injured

B   2. should have waited   3. had been blown, was scored   4. jumped   5. will be finished   6. had finished   7. strikes, will
be done   8. whipped   9. will go   10. come   11. may want, will get   12. stand, deliver

Page 17.

A   2. runs, runs, run, run   3. jumps, jumps, jumps, jump, jump   4. falls, falls, fall, fall, fall   5. hits, hits, hit, hit, hit   6. write, writes, writes, write, write   7. catches, catches, catch, catch   8. wishes, wishes, wish, wish, wish   9. tries, try, tries, try, try   10. cries, cries, cry, cry, cry

Page 19. Now test yourself

A   1. arrested   2. fought   3. kick   4. ploughed
B   1. had caught   2. will telephone   3. would climb   4. will be pleased
C   1. is   2. tastes, tastes   3. feel ill, will stay   4. are, should like, to stay
D   1. brought   2. swam   3. knelt   4. blew   5. said   6. lost
E   1. drawn   2. sold   3. laid   4. broken   5. flown   6. written
F   1. know   2. knew   3. known   4. knows   5. know   6.know

Page 20.

A   2. neatly   3. loudly   4. clearly   5. freely   6. bravely
B   2. easy   3 humble   4. gentle
C   2. early   3. fast   4. short
D   2. clumsily   3. loudly   4. slowly

Page 21.

A   2. immediately   3. today   4. seldom   5. already   6. soon
B   2. outside   3. straight   4. behind   5. out   6. above
C   2. almost   3. quite/completely   4. less   5. thoroughly   6. so

Page 22.

A   2. harder, hardest   3. faster, fastest   4. later, latest   5. earlier, earliest
B   2. more happily, most happily   3. more quickly, most quickly   4. more carefully, most carefully   5. more easily, most easily
C   2. farther, farthest   3. less, least   4. more, most   5. better, best

Page 23.

A   1. soon   2. formerly   3. quickly   4. badly   5. once   6. where
B   1. impudently   2. smartly   3. gleefully   4. greedily   5. lovingly   6. tunefully   7. fitfully   8. bitterly
C   1. more, most   2. iller, illest; or worse, worst   3. earlier, earliest   4. more, most   5. more, most   6. more, most
D   1. more quickly   2. more carefully   3. brightest   4. more closely   5. harder   6. latest

Page 24.

A   2. but   3. nor   4. or   5. but/yet
B   2. both, and   3. so, as   4. Either, or   5. Neither, nor   6. Whether, or

Page 25.

A   2.before   3. After   4. since   5. until   6. While   7. As   8. till
B   1. Where   2. Wherever   3. because   4. since   5. As
C   1. even if   2. Although   3. whether   4. unless   5. If   6. so that   7. as if   8. As … as

Page 26

A   2. to   3. towards   4. down   5. over   6. between   7. up/down   8. in   9. at
B   2/3. on/by   4/5/6. towards/between/through

Page 27

A   2. after   3. from/to   4. about
B   2. into, until   3. past   4. under
C   2. till   3. near   4. off
D   2. except for   3. due to   4. in front of   5. away from   6. on top of   7. out of   8. by means of

Page 28

A   2. Hooray!   3. Oh dear!   4. Oh!   5. Help!
B   2. Ouch   3. Oops   4. Ooh   5. Oh dear
C   the, an, a

Page 29. Now test yourself.

A   1. and   2. before   3. until   4. where   5. because   6. although (though)   7. whether   8. if   9. as if   10. so that
B   1. to   2. up   3. against   4. into   5. on   6. along   7. beneath (under, underneath)   8. through   9. round   10. over
C   1. Oh   2. Phew   3. Ouch   4. Oh   5. Hooray

Page 30. Now test yourself.

Count five points for each correct answer. You could score 200 points for all-correct answers.

Nouns A 1. girl   2. picture   3. meal   4. plate   5. chips   6. beans   7. eggs   8. sausages   9. teacher   10. class   11. paint   12. sauce.

Verbs B 1. painted   2. could show   3. had finished   4. was finished   5. showed   6. gasped   7. was covered   8. to do   9. did   10. said   11. have   12. love

Adjectives C 1. little   2. favourite   3. delicious   4. rich   5. crisp   6. baked   7. fried   8. sizzling   9. fat   10. red   11. terrible   12. tomato

Adverbs D 1. industriously   2. carefully   3. proudly   4. angrily

Punctuation

AGE 9-11

Boswell Taylor

As a parent, you can play a major role in your child's education by your interest and encouragement. This book is designed to help your child learn the basic principles of punctuation. Punctuation is a code of marks which is used to make our meaning clear when we write. Confidence in punctuation will support your child's performance in all school subjects.

Each punctuation mark is explained and then there are exercises to practise each point. These are followed by a test to check your child's understanding. Answers to all the exercises and tests are given at the back of the book.

*Hodder
Children's
Books*

NCPTA

The only home learning programme supported by the NCPTA

How to help your child

- Make sure your child completes all the exercises for each punctuation mark. Practising punctuation in context is the best way to gain confidence.

- Encourage your child to check answers by reading them aloud. The punctuation should help the words flow naturally and make the meaning clear.

- If your child gets answers wrong, talk through the explanations of the relevant points to make sure they have been fully understood. Then suggest your child has another go at the exercises.

- Remember that the use of punctuation changes gradually over the years. There is a tendency now to use less punctuation than in the past.

- Concentrate on your child's successes and give plenty of praise and encouragement.

Published by Hodder Children's Books 1995

Printed and bound in Great Britain

Hodder Children's Books
A division of Hodder Headline
338 Euston Road
London NW1 3BH

Why we need punctuation

When we talk we can do all kinds of things to make our meaning clear. We can put words into groups or separate them. We can pause for breath or effect. We can emphasize words or phrases to make them sound important. We can raise our voices to indicate that we are asking a question. We can express our feelings by exclaiming with joy or surprise or fright.

We can do none of these things when we write. We therefore use a code to make our meaning clear. The code tells the reader how to read the words we have written. This code is called punctuation and the code signs are called punctuation marks. These are the code signs. These are the punctuation marks:

.	,	?	!	'
full stop or period	comma	question mark	exclamation mark	apostrophe
—	:	;	-	( )
dash	colon	semi-colon	hyphen	brackets

" " or ' '
quotation marks or inverted commas or speech marks or lip marks

You will find these punctuation marks in letters and books. You will see them on television and computer screens, and nearly everywhere that you can see words. Without written marks of punctuation to replace speech signals, we could not make our thoughts clear. Punctuation marks help the reader to understand our ideas. Punctuation marks can give a different meaning to the words in a sentence. Look at this sentence:

What are we waiting for Lisa?

This is one meaning …   **What are we waiting for, Lisa?**
Change the punctuation marks
and we have another meaning … **What! Are we waiting for Lisa?**
Again …   **What are we waiting for?**
                               Lisa.

The punctuation code is essential to reading aloud. Try reading aloud what you have written, and then you will know if the punctuation has made your meaning clear.

A sentence begins with a capital and ends with a full stop

The full stop (or period) is the punctuation mark most frequently used.
A full stop is necessary when a speaker stops for breath.
It brings a statement or a single idea to an end.

Punctuate the following. Begin each sentence with a capital letter.
End each sentence with a full stop.
Note that the first one is done for you. (This rule applies to each exercise in the book.)

A 1 the cowboy was thrown from his horse
    The cowboy was thrown from his horse.

  2 she climbed the mountain to its snow-capped summit

  3 rockets shot into the sky

  4 we are going to the fair

  5 the tiger leapt upon the back of the frightened animal

  6 the spacecraft landed on the moon

Six sentences have been split up. Here are their endings:

netted the floundering salmon   looped the loop
hit the ball into the air   painted a picture of the barn
reached the sunken wreck   skidded round the corner

Give the correct ending for each beginning shown below:

B 1 The impatient batsman *hit the ball into the air.*

  2 The fisherman

  3 The diver

  4 The motorcyclist

  5 The brave pilot

  6 The artist

4

Full stops are used in some abbreviations

Abbreviations are the shortened form of words or phrases. They often consist of the initial letters of the words in the phrases.

Use full stops after initials in names. Write only the initials of the first names.

A 1 Frederick George Smith   Susan Joanne Edmunds
       <u>F.G.Smith</u>   <u>S.J.Edmunds</u>

   2 Write your own name in its abbreviated form.

       ....

   3 Write the abbreviated names of three people you know.

       ....

Full stops are placed after some abbreviations where the final letters of the word(s) are missing. They are also used in titles containing words that begin with both capital letters and small letters. Here are some examples:

Nov.   ch.   Prof.   k.p.h.   v.

Write the following as abbreviations.

B 1 Department of Trade ...<u>D.o.T</u>...   2 Bachelor of Science ....

   3 December ....   4 page ....

   5 Telephone ....   6 department ....

For what words or phrases are these the abbreviations?

C 1 k.p.h...<u>kilometres per hour</u>....   2 Nov. ....

   3 ch. ....   4 v. ....

Most abbreviations are now used without full stops, for example BBC, RSPCA, LBW. Mathematical and scientific terms are usually written without stops. Examples are kg, cm, ml.

Contractions which include the last letter of the original word do not have stops. Dr, Mr, Bros and St are examples. Can you find more?

Write the following as abbreviations without full stops:

D 1 British Broadcasting
       Corporation ...<u>BBC</u>...   2 millimetres ....

   3 Member of Parliament .... 4 Justice of the Peace ....

How to use capital letters

Capital letters are used to begin sentences.

Punctuate these instructions. Write in sentences using full stops and capital letters. There are five sentences:

A ask a friend to hold a coin tightly in his or her hand inform your friend that you can tell the day's date put your hand on his or her head pretend to think hard tell your friend today's date

Ask a friend to hold a coin tightly in his or her hand.
....
....
....
....
....

Capital letters are used to begin special names.
Write names which are examples of the following:

B	1 king	president	admiral
	Arthur		
	2 ship	pop group	horse
	HMS Victory		
	3 country	continent	city
	France		
	4 mountain	river	desert
	Snowdon		

Capital letters are used for 'I' (capital 'i') and to begin words in titles.
Write titles which are examples of the following:

C 1 an adventure book *The Thirty-nine Steps* ....

   2 a computer game ....

   3 a pop song ....

   4 a poem ....

   5 a television programme ....
....

Capital letters are also used to begin direct speech and lines of poetry.

★ Now test yourself (capitals and full stops)

Punctuate the sentences in A and B using the capital letter and the full stop:

A 1 the dog barked when the burglar approached

....

   2 as he passed through the laser beam the gates shut

....

   3 no one knew the answer

....

   4 the horseman was lost in a cloud of dust

....

B the prized mascot of an american regiment in germany was a buffalo
   named cross-eyes they kept it in a large cage a british regiment felt sorry
   for the animal one morning the buffalo disappeared in its place was
   an oxo cube

....

....

....

....

....

C Write this verse in five lines adding capital letters and full stops
   where necessary:
   there was an old man of kildare, who climbed into a very high chair; then
   he said,"here i stays, till the end of my days" that immovable man of kildare

....

....

....

....

....

A comma marks a brief pause in a sentence

The insertion of commas can change the meaning of a sentence:

Fiona, my friend, is riding the horse. (Fiona is riding the horse.)
Fiona, my friend is riding the horse. (Fiona is not riding the horse.)

Insert the commas in these sentences to give the meaning intended:

A 1 Carpet for sale, the property of a lady, too large for her house.
  2 The man was killed while cooking the dinner in a frightful way.
  3 Wanted: piano for a man with a patterned front and mahogany legs.
  4 The clown who knew the girl wore patched trousers and had a red nose.
  5 The mother bought a comb for the baby with plastic teeth.

In this sentence the comma has been inserted *in the wrong place*.
Rewrite the sentence correctly, with two commas:

  6 The Earl who was the chieftain of his clan wore nothing, to show
    his rank.

Commas are used to separate names in a list:

**Children go to school on Monday, Tuesday, Wednesday, Thursday
and Friday.**

Answer the following questions in sentences, choosing the correct items from
each list.

B 1 Which three are birds?   wrens, robins, zebras, fawns, swifts
     Wrens, robins and swifts are birds.
....

  2 Which three are flowers?   roses, pearls, whelks, pinks, tulips

     ....

  3 Which three are furniture?   tables, attics, divans, anoraks, sofas

     ....

  4 Which three are fruits?   apricots, goblets, pears, tangos, plums

     ....

  5 Which three are drinks?   nectarines, milk, wagtails, coffee, tea

     ....

Commas may be used to separate a sequence of actions or instructions:

**Climb the hill, cross the river, walk along the lane and you will reach
the farm.**

We use commas to divide numbers **(5,683,542)** but not in dates **(1983)**.
In high numbers we sometimes use a space instead of a comma.

★ Now test yourself (commas)

Punctuate the following, inserting commas where necessary.

A 1 The farther he travelled the more weary he became.
2 I will go but you will stay here.
3 The deeper you dig however the wetter the ground becomes.
4 Before the fire brigade arrived the house was burnt to the ground.
5 First I would like to know which school you attend.
6 Yes I am much better today.
7 Jane Powell my best friend will be there to meet me.
8 Stand in front of me Jonathan and let me take a good look at you.
9 The prisoner wounded though he was managed to escape.
10 There are 52678391 people living in the country.

Answer the following questions in sentences. Choose the correct items.

B 1 Which three are cities?   Manchester, Vietnam, Bonn, Oslo, Sweden

....

2 Which three are games?   chess, granite, baseball, baskets, tennis

....

3 Which three are insects?   ants, earwigs, weasels, eels, termites

....

4 Which three are   barometers, oboes, guitars, violins, buoys
musical instruments?

....

5 Which three are minerals?   sonatas, zinc, iron, tungsten, migraines

....

To help you   Commas are used to help the reader, not to confuse him or her.
They indicate a pause or a change in the expression or tone of voice. Try
reading the sentences aloud (or nearly so) noting when you pause or
change your tone of voice.
There is a tendency for fewer commas to be used nowadays, but they
should always be used if they make the meaning clearer for the reader.

When to use the question mark

When we ask a question we use a special tone of voice.
When we write a question we use a question mark (?).
A question usually expects an answer.

The question mark is used only when an actual direct question is asked:

What is your name?   **When will you be able to go?**

Write answers to these questions:

A 1 When do leaves fall from trees?

Leaves fall _in the Autumn._ ....

  2 Where do rooks build their nests?

Rooks build ....

  3 Why does a hedgehog have prickles?

A hedgehog has ....

  4 Which animal has tusks and a trunk?

.... has tusks and a trunk.

  5 How does a cricket chirp?

A cricket chirps by ....

  6 What is the favourite food of the squirrel?

The favourite food ....

Write questions which could give these answers:

B 1 _What time does the bus leave?_ ....

The bus leaves at noon.

  2 ....

The kiwi lives in New Zealand.

  3 ....

Paris is the capital of France.

  4 ....

The disco is held on Thursday evenings.

Questions often begin with **What ... ? When ... ? Why ... ? Where ... ? How ... ?**

Use the question mark after a single word that indicates a question.

Why?   How?   Where?   When?   What?

The question mark is used after a statement followed by a short question:

It never rains but it pours, does it?

Notice the comma before the question.

Add the short questions appropriate to the following statements.

A 1 You are not the tallest girl in the class, *are you?* ....

2 April is not the wettest month, ...

3 You can't grow onions in mud, ...

4 We will not climb to the top of the mountain, ...

5 You will try harder next time, ...

6 It's cold outside, ...

This is the report you gave to the police after you escaped from a gang of kidnappers. Write down the actual questions you were asked.

The gang asked me my nationality. They wanted to know my name. They asked me why I was visiting the island. They wanted to know how much money I had. They asked if my parents were rich. They asked if they would pay a ransom for me.

B 1 *What is your nationality?* ....

2 ....

3 ....

4 ....

5 ....

6 ....

Punctuate the following:

C 1 SON   Dad ☐ what has a black and red striped body ☐ two great eyes on stalks ☐ six hairy legs and a long proboscis ☐

       FATHER   I don't know ☐ Why ☐

       SON   One has just settled on your bald patch ☐

2 LADY   Do you charge for bread ☐

       WAITER   No ☐

       LADY   Do you charge for gravy ☐

       WAITER   No ☐

       LADY   May I have two slices of bread with gravy ☐ please ☐

How to use the exclamation mark

The exclamation mark (!) should be used with caution. Well selected words can often do the same job. A spatter of exclamation marks on a page will irritate a reader. If in doubt – miss out.

The exclamation mark is used to express strong or sudden feelings:
   Help!   Good for you!   Oh!   That hurts!

It can be used to emphasize a command or a strong viewpoint:
   Go away!   Attention!   I don't want to talk about it!

It can be used to show irony, sarcasm or amusement:
   What a funny girl you are!   You are the last one to talk about envy!

Exclamation marks can follow sentences, words or phrases. It acts as a full stop, so the next word always begins with a capital letter.

Punctuate, using exclamation marks or question marks:

A 1 Oh dear are you going away
   Oh dear! Are you going away?
   ....

   2 Help it stings where is the ointment
   ....

   3 Get off the grass can't you see that it is wet
   ....

   4 Hurry up do you think you are the only person who wants to try
   ....

   5 Stop it I don't want to hear anything about it
   ....

   6 Let go what do you think you are doing I won't stop
   ....

Punctuate with one full stop, one question mark and two exclamation marks:

B   "My dog's got no nose ☐"
      "Poor dog ☐ How does he smell ☐"
      "Awful ☐ "

★ Now test yourself (question marks and exclamation marks)

Punctuate the following, inserting question marks and exclamation marks:

1 Where did you find the owl with the broken wing

   ....

2 Don't make me laugh

   ....

3 You are the most remarkable person I have ever met

   ....

4 Am I invited to your party Do you really want me to come

   ....

5 Will you come to me immediately I said immediately

   ....

6 Oh Why did you creep so quietly up to me You are frightening

   ....

7 Dear Dear Why don't you hit the nail instead of my finger

   ....

8 Goodness gracious me Look at the time Shouldn't we be going

   ....

9 Knock Knock Who's there

   ....

10 What are you doing That hurts

   ....

11 Where are you hiding Come out at once

   ....

12 Now Now You have forgotten

   ....

To help you   The question mark and the exclamation mark suggest a tone of voice. Try reading the sentences aloud. Question marks are only used when a direct question is asked. Do not over-use exclamation marks. Ration them.

How to use quotation marks

Quotation marks are sometimes single (' '), and sometimes double (" ").
They are sometimes called inverted commas, speech marks or lip marks.

Quotation marks indicate the actual (and exact) words spoken or quoted:
> **"The pirates will all hang," said the captain.**
> **The captain said, "The pirates will all hang."**

Notice the comma separating the actual words spoken from the rest.

Quotation marks go round each part of a direct quotation if it is broken up:
> **"The pirates," said the captain, "will all hang."**

Notice the commas separating the actual words spoken from the rest:
> **," said the captain,"**

Notice also that, as the quotation is a broken sentence, the second part does not begin with a capital letter.

The quotation may consist of more than one sentence:
> **"The pirates will all hang," said the captain. "They are all criminals.**
> **They have killed many sailors. They must die."**

Punctuate the following using quotation marks. All the other kinds of punctuation are given.

A 1 Oh dear! I have lost my way, said the instructor, and I don't know which way to go.

"Oh dear! I have lost my way, " said the instructor, "and I don't know which way to go."

2 I hit the ball over the wall, said the boy, and we can't find it.

....

....

3 Stop that thief! cried the old lady.

....

....

4 Kate said firmly, I want my banana now, Grannie.

....

....

5 Ah! I recognise you now, said the shopkeeper. Aren't you the man who gave me a fake five pound note?

....

....

Punctuate the following using quotation marks.
The other kinds of punctuation are given.

B 1 I have lost my memory, said the patient.
       When did that happen? asked the doctor.
       When did what happen? said the patient.

   2 We have a hen, said Jackie, that lays brown eggs.
      Well, what is so wonderful about that? asked Meg.
      Could you do it? asked Jackie.

   3 A boy was swimming in a private pool. The owner saw him and was very
      annoyed. He shouted to the boy, You can't swim in this pool. It's private.
      The boy answered, I am not swimming. I am only trying to stop
      myself sinking.

These are reported conversations. Using quotation marks, write out the actual
words spoken:

C 1 Jerry asked Tom how he had got on in the milk-drinking competition.
      Tom answered that he had won by three laps.

      ....

      ....

      ....

      ....

   2 My mother said that Maggie knew that she must not eat with a knife.
      Maggie replied that she did know, but her fork leaked!

      ....

      ....

      ....

      ....

   3 Write a story of your own using quotation marks.

How to use the apostrophe 1

The apostrophe (') is used to show possession.

John's bat = the bat that belongs to John

Jilly's bike = the bike that belongs to Jilly

Rule One   In the singular (referring to only one owner) use the apostrophe + s.

Make the following possessive, using the apostrophe:

A 1 the spade of the gardener ......*the gardener's spade*......

   2 the cow of the farmer ....

   3 the tape-recorder of the teacher ....

   4 the ring of the bride ....

   5 the song of the thrush ....

   6 the engine of the car ....

Rule Two   In the plural (referring to more than one owner) add the apostrophe only *when the plural ends in ------s or -------es:*

B 1 the pencils of the boys ......*the boys' pencils*......

   2 the sails of the boats ....

   3 the bells of the churches ....

   4 the ears of the donkeys ....

   5 the shields of the squires ....

   6 the hats of the ladies ....

Rule Three   When the plural does not end in -s add the apostrophe +s:

C 1 the boots of the policemen ......*the policemen's boots*......

   2 the anoraks of the men ....

   3 the homework of the children ....

   4 the cars of the women ....

Caution   Some words showing possession *never* take an apostrophe. They are:

   its   hers   his   ours   yours   theirs

      The snake raised its head and showed its fangs.
....

D Write a sentence for each of the words above, similar to the example. Do not use an apostrophe.

Write the following sentences making use of the apostrophe to show possession. The words to be changed are shown in **bold type**:

E 1 The **coats of the ladies** were taken to the cloakroom.
       The ladies' coats were taken to the cloakroom.
   ....

   2 The books were placed on the **desk of the librarian**.

   ....

   3 The mud was solid on the **boots of the workmen**.

   ....

   4 **The head of my brother** was bruised from the blow.

   ....

   5 The burglar broke into **the house of Mr Brown**.

   ....

   6 From the display the shop evidently sold **the clothes of babies**.

   ....

   7 **The voices of women** made themselves heard.

   ....

   8 The teacher was pleased with **the interest of the parents**.

   ....

   9 The family had a **holiday of three months**.

   ....

   10 Call at **the shop of Mrs Smith** on the way back.

   ....

In the following sentences insert the correct pronouns from the list.
Do not insert apostrophes: its   hers   his   ours   yours   theirs

F 1 We like our teacher; they don't like ..*theirs*..............
   2 Your front door is red; we decided to paint .... blue.
   3 The tree sheds .... leaves in autumn.
   4 The knight returned .... sword to the scabbard.
   5 I still have my sweets; you have eaten ....

How to use the apostrophe 2

The apostrophe (') is used to show that letters have been omitted when two (or more) words have been run together to make an abbreviation:

did not didn't   **we will we'll**   **shall not shan't**

Abbreviate these phrases to make one word with an apostrophe in each case:

A 1 all is ....*all's*........   2 you are .... 3 I am ....

   4 that is ....   5 there is .... 6 he is ....

   7 did not ....   8 does not .... 9 do not ....

  10 would not ....   11 have not ....12 should not ....

Abbreviate these phrases. You should omit more than one letter in each case.

B 1 you will ......*you'll*......   2 will not .... 3 shall not ....

   4 he would ....   5 she will .... 6 I would ....

   7 we have ....   8 I have .... 9 they will ....

  10 who have ....   11 I will ....12 of the clock ....

Write these words as phrases of more than one word and without apostrophes:

C 1 can't ....*can not*.......   2 it's .... 3 isn't ....

   4 I'd ....   5 he'd .... 6 he'll ....

   7 we've ....   8 they'll .... 9 we'll ....

  10 she'll ....   11 won't ....12 who's ....

  13 wasn't ....   14 daren't ....15 mustn't ....

  16 you've ....   17 we're ....18 who've ....

Abbreviations such as those shown above are used in speech and dialogue. The words are usually written in full in formal and polite letters and in text books.

The *o* is used in *won't* because *wol* was the old form of *will*.
Use the apostrophe in *it's* only when it means *it is*.

Write the following sentences making use of the apostrophe as an abbreviation. The words to be changed are shown in **bold type**:

D 1 **We will** arrive at six **of the clock**.

....

2 **I am** too clever and **have not** been trapped yet.

....

3 Although **it is** time to go **I will** stay a little longer.

....

4 **All is** well with us and **that is** as it should be.

....

5 Now **we have** fallen off our bikes **they will** win.

....

6 **You will** be recognised everywhere now that **you are** famous.

....

7 **There is** nowhere **you are** welcome with that frown.

....

8 We **shall not** know the result until **you have** returned.

....

9 We **do not** want to go and we **will not** go.

....

10 I **shall not** forget the way **you have** helped me.

....

11 **I would** be delighted if **you would** keep the money.

....

12 Where **there is** a will **there is** a way.

....

13 **Do not** tell me **you have** lost your shorts.

....

How to use hyphens, dashes and brackets

The hyphen (-) is used to mark the division of a word at the end of a line: always divide a word only between syllables. **Al-ways** is an example.

Hyphens are used in some compound words. They separate or join the words.

Insert the hyphen in the following:

A 1 son-in-law   2 vice president   3 co operative

   4 Anglo Saxon   5 hour long   6 old fashioned

Hyphens are used in numbers between 21 and 99, and in fractions:

B 1 thirty-four   2 seventy eight   3 twenty nine

   4 two thirds   5 three quarters   6 seven eighths

Dashes — which look like these — and brackets (which look like these) are used to show an aside in a sentence or for extra information to be given. A single dash may be used before an added thought at the end of a sentence. Brackets (sometimes called parentheses) enclose information and are used in pairs.

Insert dashes — wherever necessary — in the following:

C 1 You may   although I shall be surprised if you do   enjoy this music.
   2 The 'Mary Rose'   that noble ship   sank before the eyes of the king.
   3 Jonathan Thomson   if his brother cannot come   will join us at the fair.
   4 The towels   if they are not too wet   will be used to sit on.
   5 I will try   and I will go on trying   until I succeed.
   6 The sharks were man-eaters   or so I believed.

Insert brackets (parentheses) in the following. Enclose figures and references:

D 1 I used an axe   a large one   to split the wood.
   2 The stamp   showing Queen Victoria's head   was stuck to the document.
   3 One section in the book   Chapter 2   describes the spacecraft.
   4 Can you let me have twenty-five   25   pounds?
   5 I will give you eleven   11   copies of the poem.
   6 The largest crater is about 700 miles   1100 kilometres   wide.

How to use colons and semi-colons

The colon (:) is a mark of anticipation. It starts a list or introduces a quotation.

Insert the colon in the following:

A 1 Campers must bring these items: sleeping-bags, ground-sheets and food.
   2 These are capital cities Paris, Moscow, London and Vienna.
   3 The City of Birmingham has a motto Forward.
   4 Three motorways are closed M4, M1 and M5.
   5 Three drinks are served cocoa, coffee and Coca-Cola.
   6 I have three favourite teams Aston Villa, Arsenal and Norwich.

A semi-colon (;) marks a pause in a sentence. It is stronger than a comma; it is not as strong as a full stop. A semi-colon (;) may be used instead of a conjunction like 'and' or 'but'.

Insert the semi-colon in the following:

B 1 Look at the map; check the route.
   2 Sean works hard Jack plays all day long.
   3 The king smiled kindly at Siobhan one could see he was pleased.
   4 I will read the story when I come to the end you will know why.
   5 The brother was quieter he entered the world of his books.
   6 At noon I left everybody had left.

Sometimes a semi-colon is used after a group of words in a sentence.
Insert the semi-colons in the following:

C 1 Sirens blared; bells rang; whistles shrieked; and people cheered.
   2 The engine spluttered it stopped it started again then it stopped completely.
   3 The prisoner jumped the wall he ran across the field he disappeared.

A semi-colon is used between items which contain commas.
Insert the semi-colons in the following:

D 1 The group consisted of three girls: Michelle, lead guitarist; Jane, bass guitarist; and Jacqueline, drummer.
   2 Three boys were key players: Darren, striker Peter, goalkeeper and Sam, sweeper.

★ Now test yourself (capitals and full stops)

Punctuate the following. The punctuation marks you need are shown on the right. Cross out each mark as you use it. You should use these and no more:

| 1 | MOTHER: | "Don't pull faces at the bulldog." | " " ' . / |
| | SON: | "But, mother, he started it!" | " " , . ! / |

| 2 | PATIENT: | What can you give me for my flat feet | " " ? |
| | DOCTOR: | What about a foot pump | " " - ! |

| 3 | ONLOOKER: | Why are you rolling the potato patch | " " ? |
| | GARDENER: | I m trying to grow mashed potatoes | " " ' . |

| 4 | DINER: | What has happened to this egg | " " ? |
| | WAITRESS: | I don t know madam I only laid the table | " " ' , , . |

| 5 | DINER: | Do you serve ducklings here | " " ? |
| | WAITER: | We serve anybody sir Sit down | " " , . ! |

| 6 | STUDENT: | How do you make a sausage roll | " " ? |
| | FRIEND: | That s easy Just turn it over and over | " " ' ! . |

7	FATHER:	How do you know your teacher loves you	" " ?
	GIRL:	She puts kisses next to each sum I do	
		There	" " ! .

| 8 | PATIENT: | Doctor I feel as limp as a pair of curtains | " " , . |
| | DOCTOR: | You had better pull yourself together then | " " . |

| 9 | SHOPPER: | I don t like the look of that codfish It s bad | " " ' ' . ! |
| | FISHMONGER: | If it s looks you want why not buy a goldfish | " " ' , ? |

| 10 | VICAR: | Your brother is very small isn t he | " " , ' ? |
| | BOY: | Well vicar you see he is only my half brother | " " , , , . - |

11	CUSTOMER:	This is a second hand shop isn t it	" " - , ' ?
	ASSISTANT:	Yes	" " .
	CUSTOMER:	That s lucky Please fit one on my watch	" " ' ! .

| 12 | FRIEND: | So you ve lost your dog Why don t you advertise | " " . ' ? |
| | DOG-OWNER: | Don t be silly My dog can t read | " " ' ! ' . |

22

13	BROTHER:	Well Kate how do you like school	" " , , ?
	SISTER:	Closed	" " !
14	GRETA:	I ve changed my mind	" " ' .
	CLARE:	Does the new mind work any better	" " ?
15	MOTHER:	Have you filled the salt cellar yet Nesta	" " , ?
	NESTA:	No mother it s so hard getting it through the holes	" " , , ' .
16	CUSTOMER:	May I try on this dress in the window	" " ?
	ASSISTANT:	I think you should use the dressing room madam	" " , .
17	JUSTIN:	Who gave you that black eye	" " ?
	KENNY:	Nobody gave it me I had to fight for it	" " ; .
18	CUSTOMER:	I d like to buy some crocodile shoes	" " ' .
	ASSISTANT:	What size does your crocodile take	" " ?
19	PASSENGER:	Those people down there look just like ants	" " .
	AIR STEWARD:	They are ants we haven t left the ground yet	" " — ' .
20	CAR DRIVER:	Sorry I ve killed your cat I ll replace it	" " ' . ' .
	OLD LADY:	But how well can you catch mice	" " ?
21	BOX OFFICE GIRL:	That s the third ticket you ve bought	" " ' ' .
	CINEMA-GOER:	I know a girl inside keeps tearing them up	" " ; .
22	MANAGER:	Why do you want to work in a bank	" " ?
	APPLICANT:	I understand there s money in it	" " ' .
23	SNAKE-CHARMER:	Careful There s a ten foot snake in that box	" " ! ' - .
	PORTER:	You can t kid me snakes don t have feet	" " ' — ' !
24	BRIDE:	Antony wake up I heard a mouse squeak	" " , ! .
	GROOM:	What do you want me to do get up and oil it	" " — ?

Story Section

These are the punctuation marks: comma (,), full stop or period (.), quotation marks or inverted commas (" " or ' '), exclamation mark (!), question mark (?), apostrophe ('), and hyphen (-).

These stories lack their punctuation signs. Insert the correct punctuation mark in each space indicated by ☐. You may find it helpful to read the stories aloud.

1 A woman whose family kept many pets
   looked out of her window one day when
   she heard knocking at the door☐
   A boy stood there☐
   ☐Can I help you☐☐she asked☐
   ☐Not me☐☐he replied☐☐but
   there☐s a rabbit on your doorstep
   and I don☐t think he can reach the bell☐☐

2 A motorist had trouble with his car☐ He called
   at a garage☐A mechanic looked at the engine☐
   ☐H☐m☐It☐ll take about £100 to get it
   purring again☐☐he said☐
   ☐Oh dear☐☐ exclaimed the motorist☐
   ☐How much will it cost just to get it
   to miaow a little☐☐

3 Two birds perched on a tree not far from
   an airport☐Suddenly a jet plane screamed across
   the sky☐
   ☐Did you see that☐☐said one bird☐☐I☐ve
   never seen a bird fly as fast as that☐☐
   The other bird said☐☐I bet you☐d go as fast
   as that if your tail was on fire☐☐

24

4 Peter and Paul were friends☐They often played
together on their bikes☐Peter especially
liked to ride on his friend☐s shining new
bike☐One day Peter called for Paul☐
☐I☐m sorry☐Peter☐☐said his friend☐s
mother☐☐Paul can☐t come out this morning☐☐
☐Oh☐☐said Peter☐looking disappointed☐
Then he brightened up☐☐Can his new bike
come out instead☐☐he said☐

5 Joanna had just begun school and☐already☐
she thought she could read and write☐ One day
her mother saw her scribbling on some paper☐
☐What are you drawing☐☐she asked☐
☐I☐m not drawing☐☐ said Joanna
indignantly☐☐I am writing a letter to
Sara☐☐
☐But you can☐t write☐☐said her mother☐
☐That☐s all right☐☐said Joanna☐☐Sara
can☐t read☐☐

Can you explain the point of each story? You may like to draw a picture by the
side of each story. There are some more stories to punctuate on the next four
pages.

6 A lion and a lioness were asleep in their
cage☐much to the disappointment of a boy who
was visiting the zoo with his father☐The man
put a coin in the tape☐recorder machine☐
As the boy listened to the description of the
animal☐the lion rolled over☐yawned☐then
stood up and roared loudly☐
The boy☐delighted☐pointed to the still☐
sleeping lioness☐
He shouted☐☐Put another in the box☐Dad☐☐

7 A sword☐swallower was demonstrating his
skill☐He swallowed some pins and nails☐
☐Oh☐Oh☐ scoffed the onlookers☐☐Those
aren☐t swords☐They☐re only pins
and nails☐☐
☐Well☐you see☐☐said the sword☐swallower☐
☐I☐m on a diet☐☐

8 A young pigeon was allowed to fly out by himself
for the first time☐He just managed to get home
with his feathers bedraggled☐his tail
plucked☐and his wings limp☐
☐Whatever has happened☐☐ asked his mother☐
☐It☐s not my fault☐☐moaned the young pigeon☐
☐I flew down to see what game two girls were
playing☐☐
☐What were they playing☐☐asked his mother☐
☐Badminton☐☐said the young pigeon☐☐and☐
before I knew where I was☐I was the
shuttle☐cock☐☐

9 The family had been to the circus□They all
seemed impressed by the knife□thrower except
Timothy□
□I thought he was very clever□□said Father□
□He was no good at all□□said Timothy□
□I don□t know how you can say that□□said
his father□ Look at how fast and furiously
he threw those knives at the girl□□
□But he missed every time□□exclaimed
Timothy□

10 A competition for the biggest pumpkin was held
at a youth club□
A notice was put on the peg board□
□Pumpkin Contest□□it said□
□All those interested please sign below□□
Among the signatures was written the name
□Cinderella□□

11 A dignified gentleman□who did not like
children□was enjoying a quiet read in a very
silent library□Suddenly a class of noisy
young children came in□They were very
excited and they were very noisy□
Finally the dignified gentleman could stand
the noise no longer□He called the teacher to
him□When she returned to the class she said□
□Will you all make less noise□That gentleman
says that he can□t read□□
□Then he should be ashamed of himself□□
said one girl□□ I could read when I was
only five years old□□

12 A man was taking a stroll through the park
   when a penguin suddenly appeared in front
   of him□He took the penguin to the park□
   keeper and said□□I□ve found this penguin□
   What shall I do□□
   The keeper suggested that he take the penguin to
   the zoo□
   The next day the park□keeper met the same man
   still with the penguin□He walked up to him□
   □Didn□t I tell you to take the penguin to
   the zoo□□ he said□
   □Yes□□ replied the man□□and that□s what
   I did yesterday□I□m taking him to the cinema
   today□□

13 A policeman in the park saw a duck which had
   strayed from the pool□He caught it□tied
   a piece of string round its neck and led it
   back to the pool□
   He met two boys□They stared at him amazed□
   □What do you think of that□□said one boy□
   □They must have run out of police dogs□□

14 A farmer decided that his horse was overfed
   by people passing through the field□He placed
   a notice on the gate□
   □Please do not give this horse tit□bits□
   Signed□The Owner□□
   A few days later he was surprised to see
   another notice on the gate below his own□
   It read□□Please do not pay attention to
   the above notice□Signed□The Horse□□

15 A teacher was telling her class the story of
   Noah and his ark□They were very impressed at
   the thought of all the animals going into the
   ark two by two□
   □What do you think they did when they were
   all in the ark□□asked the teacher□
   There was silence□
   □All right□What do you think Noah did□□she then asked□
   □Fished□□said one girl□
   □What□□exclaimed a young fisherman□
   □With only two worms□□

16 A lion was roaring his way across the jungle
   when he saw a wild pig□He roared□
   □Who is the king of the jungle□□
   □You are□□squeaked the pig□
   The lion went on his way and met a deer□
   He roared□□Who is the king of the jungle□□
   □You are□□answered the deer□
   Once more the lion went on his way□
   He came upon an elephant□He roared□
   □Who is the king of the jungle□□
   The elephant picked the lion up with his
   trunk□swung him round and threw him to
   the ground□The lion picked himself up□
   □All right□All right□□he said□
   □There□s no need to get mad because you
   don□t know the answer□□

Answers

Page 4
A 2   She climbed the mountain to its snow-capped summit.

     3   Rockets shot into the sky.

     4   We are going to the fair.

     5   The tiger leapt upon the back of the frightened animal.

     6   The spacecraft landed on the moon.

B 2   The fisherman netted the floundering salmon.

     3   The diver reached the sunken wreck.

     4   The motorcyclist skidded round the corner.

     5   The brave pilot looped the loop.

     6   The artist painted a picture of the barn.

Page 5
B 2 B.Sc.   3 Dec.   4 p.   5 Tel.   6 dept.

C 2 November   3 chapter   4 versus

D 2 mm   3 MP   4 JP

Page 6
A Inform your friend that you can tell the day's date. Put your hand on his or her head.

    Pretend to think hard. Tell your friend today's date.

Page 7
A 1   The dog barked when the burglar approached.

     2   As he passed through the laser beam the gates shut.

     3   No one knew the answer.

     4   The horseman was lost in a cloud of dust.

B The prized mascot of an American regiment in Germany was a buffalo named Cross-eyes. They kept it in a large cage. A British regiment felt sorry for the animal. One morning the buffalo disappeared. In its place was an Oxo cube.

There was an old man of Kildare,/Who climbed into a very high chair; /Then he said,"Here I stays, / Till the end of my days."/That immovable man of Kildare.

Page 8
A 2   The man was killed, while cooking the dinner, in a frightful way.

     3   Wanted: piano for a man, with a patterned front and mahogany legs.

     4   The clown, who knew the girl, wore patched trousers and had a red nose.

     5   The mother bought a comb for the baby, with plastic teeth.

     6   The Earl, who was the chieftain of his clan, wore nothing to show his rank.

B 2   Roses, pinks and tulips are flowers.

     3   Tables, divans and sofas are furniture.

     4   Apricots, pears and plums are fruits.

     5   Milk, tea and coffee are drinks.

Page 9
A 1   The farther he travelled, the more weary he became. 2 I will go, but you will stay here. 3 The deeper you dig, however, the wetter the ground becomes.   4 Before the fire brigade arrived, the house was burnt to the ground.   5 First, I would like to know which school you attend.   6 Yes, I am much better today. 7 Jane Powell, my best friend, will be there to meet me. 8 Stand in front of me, Jonathan, and let me take a good look at you. 9 The prisoner, wounded though he was, managed to escape.   10 There are 52,678,391 people living in the country.

B 1   Manchester, Bonn and Oslo are cities. 2 Chess, baseball and tennis are games.

     3   Ants, earwigs and termites are insects. 4 Oboes, guitars and violins are musical instruments.

     5   Zinc, iron and tungsten are minerals.

Page 10
A Accept any answers which start with a capital letter and end with a full stop.

B 2 Where does the kiwi live?   3 What is the capital of France?   4 When is the disco held?

Page 11

A 2 is it?   3 can you?   4 will we?   5 won't you?   6 isn't it?

B 2 What is your name?   3 Why are you visiting the island?   4 How much money do you have?
   5 Are your parents rich?   6 Will they pay a ransom for you?

C 1 ,,,?.?!   2 ?.?.,?

Page 12

A 2 Help, it stings! Where is the ointment?   3 Get off the grass! Can't you see that it is wet?
   4 Hurry up! Do you think you are the only person who wants to try?   5 Stop it! I don't want to
   hear anything about it!   6 Let go! What do you think you are doing? I won't stop!

B .!?!

Page 13

1 Where did you find the owl with the broken wing?   2 Don't make me laugh!   3 You are the most
   remarkable person I have ever met!   4 Am I invited to your party? Do you really want me to come?

5 Will you come to me immediately? I said immediately!   6 Oh! Why did you creep so quietly up to me?
   You are frightening!   7 Dear! Dear! Why don't you hit the nail instead of my finger?   8 Goodness
   gracious me! Look at the time! Shouldn't we be going?   9 Knock! Knock! Who's there?   10 What are
   you doing? That hurts!   11 Where are you hiding? Come out at once!   12 Now! Now! You have
   forgotten!

Page 14

2 "I hit the ball over the wall," said the boy, "and we can't find it."   3 "Stop that thief!" cried the old lady.

4 Kate said firmly, "I want my banana now, Grannie."   5 "Ah! I recognise you now," said the shopkeeper.
   "Aren't you the man who gave me a fake five pound note?"

Page 15

B 1 "I have lost my memory," said the patient.   "When did that happen?" asked the doctor.
      "When did what happen?" said the patient.

   2 "We have a hen," said Jackie, "that lays brown eggs." "Well, what is so wonderful about that?" asked
      Meg. "Could you do it?" asked Jackie.

   3 A boy was swimming in a private pool. The owner saw him and was very annoyed. He shouted to the
      boy, "You can't swim in this pool. It's private." The boy answered, "I am not swimming. I am only trying
      to stop myself sinking."

C 1 "Tom, how did you get on in the milk-drinking competition?" "I won by three laps."

C 2 "Maggie, you know you must not eat with a knife." "I know, but my fork leaks!"

Page 16

A 2 the farmer's cow   3 the teacher's tape-recorder   4 the bride's ring   5 the thrush's song
   6 the car's engine

B 2 the boats' sails   3 the churches' bells   4 the donkeys' ears   5 the squires' shields
   6 the ladies' hats

C 2 the men's anoraks   3 the children's homework   4 the women's cars

Page 17

E 2 the librarian's desk   3 the workmen's boots   4 My brother's head   5 Mr Brown's house
   6 babies' clothes   7 The women's voices   8 the parents' interest   9 three months' holiday
   10 Mrs Smith's shop

F 2 ours   3 its   4 his   5 yours

Page 18

A 2 you're   3 I'm   4 that's   5 there's   6 he's   7 didn't   8 doesn't   9 don't
   10 wouldn't   11 haven't   12 shouldn't

B 2 won't   3 shan't   4 he'd   5 she'll   6 I'd   7 we've   8 I've   9 they'll
   10 who've   11 I'll   12 o'clock

C 2 it is   3 is not   4 I had/I would   5 he had/he would   6 he will   7 we have   8 they will
   9 we shall   10 she will   11 will not   12 who is/has   13 was not   14 dare not   15 must not
   16 you have   17 we are   18 who have

Page 19

D 1 We'll, o'clock   2 I'm, haven't   3 it's, I'll   4 All's, that's   5 we've, they'll   6 You'll, you're
   7 There's, you're   8 shan't, you've   9 don't, won't   10 shan't, you've   11 I'd, you'd
   12 there's, there's   13 Don't, you've

Page 20

A 2 vice-president 3 co-operative 4 Anglo-Saxon 5 hour-long 6 old-fashioned

B 2 seventy-eight 3 twenty-nine 4 two-thirds 5 three-quarters 6 seven-eighths

C 1 – although I shall be surprised if you do – 2 – that noble ship – 3 – if his brother cannot come –
    4 – if they are not too wet – 5 – and I will go on trying – 6 – or so I believed.

D 1 (a large one) 2 (showing Queen Victoria's head) 3 (Chapter 2) 4 (25)
    5 (11) 6 (1100 kilometres)

Page 21

A 2 after "cities" 3 after "motto" 4 4 after "closed" 5 after "served" 6 after "teams"

B 2 after "hard" 3 after "Siobhan" 4 after "story" 5 after "quieter" 6 after first "left"

C 2 The engine spluttered; it stopped; it started again; then it stopped completely.
    3 The prisoner jumped the wall; he ran across the field; he disappeared.

D 2 Three boys were key players: Darren, striker; Peter, goalkeeper; and Sam, sweeper.

Page 22–23

2 "What can you give me for my flat feet?" "What about a foot-pump!" 3 "Why are you rolling the potato patch?" "I'm trying to grow mashed potatoes." 4 "What has happened to this egg?" "I don't know, madam, I only laid the table." 5 "Do you serve ducklings here?" "We serve anybody, sir. Sit down!" 6 "How do you make a sausage roll?" "That's easy! Just turn it over and over." 7 "How do you know your teacher loves you?" "She puts kisses next to each sum I do. There!" 8 "Doctor, I feel as limp as a pair of curtains." "You had better pull yourself together then." 9 "I don't like the look of that codfish. It's bad!" "If it's looks you want, why not buy a goldfish?" 10 "Your brother is very small, isn't he?" "Well, vicar, you see, he is only my half-brother." 11 "This is a second-hand shop, isn't it?" "Yes." "That's lucky! Please fit one on my watch."
12 "So you've lost your dog. Why don't you advertise?" "Don't be silly! My dog can't read."13 "Well, Kate, how do you like school?" "Closed!" 14 "I've changed my mind." "Does the new mind work any better?"
15 "Have you filled the salt cellar yet, Nesta?" "No, mother, it's so hard getting it through the holes."
16 "May I try on this dress in the window?" "I think you should use the dressing room, madam."
17 "Who gave you that black eye?" "Nobody gave it me; I had to fight for it." 18 "I'd like to buy some crocodile shoes." "What size does your crocodile take?" 19 "Those people down there look just like ants." "They are ants – we haven't left the ground yet." 20 "Sorry I've killed your cat. I'll replace it." "But how well can you catch mice?" 21 "That's the third ticket you've bought." "I know; a girl inside keeps tearing them up." 22 "Why do you want to work in a bank?" "I understand there's money in it." 23 "Careful! There's a ten-foot snake in that box." "You can't kid me – snakes don't have feet!" 24 "Antony, wake up! I heard a mouse squeak." "What do you want me to do – get up and oil it?"

Pages 24-29

Unfortunately, space does not permit us to include answers to the story section.

Reasoning

AGE 9-11

Alastair Pollitt

As a parent, you can play a major role in your child's education by your interest and encouragement. This book is designed to help improve your child's performance in the kinds of test commonly used for school selection and entrance examinations. By practising the various types of reasoning exercise at home, your child will become more confident in tackling them under examination conditions.

It is divided into five sections, each dealing with a particular kind of reasoning:

A   Picture Reasoning
B   Verbal Reasoning: Problems
C   Verbal Reasoning: Symbols
D   Verbal Reasoning: Concepts
E   Non-verbal Reasoning

Answers to all the questions are given at the back of the book.

Hodder
Children's
Books

NCPTA

The only home learning programme supported by the NCPTA

How to help your child

- Explain calmly to your child what has to be done in each section and make sure he or she understands how to record the answers.

- This book can be used purely for practice. However, if you wish to use it to simulate test conditions, you should set time limits as follows: 25 minutes for Section A, 40 minutes each for Sections B to D, and 30 minutes for Section E.

- If your child gets answers wrong, talk through the questions and try to find out if a particular type of question causes more problems than others. If so, concentrate on practising this type.

- Make sure that both you and your child approach this book as an enjoyable challenge, rather than an unpleasant chore. Concentrate on your child's successes and give plenty of praise and encouragement.

Published by Hodder Children's Books 1995

Printed and bound in Great Britain

Hodder Children's Books
A division of Hodder Headline
338 Euston Road
London NW1 3BH

Previously published as Test Your Child's Reasoning Ability

A. Picture Reasoning

Draw a line through the picture which doesn't belong to the set.

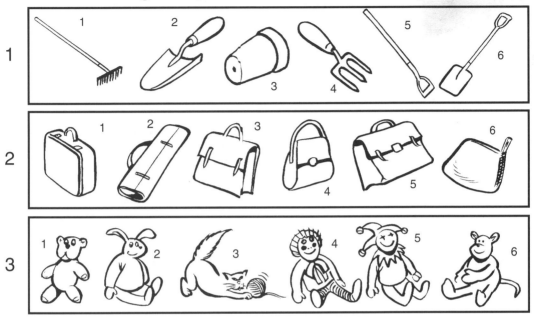

Draw a line through the picture which has something wrong with it.

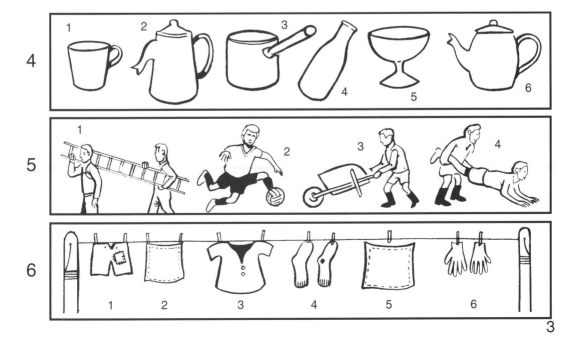

↓ is to ↓ as ↓ is to .....Draw a line through *one* picture.

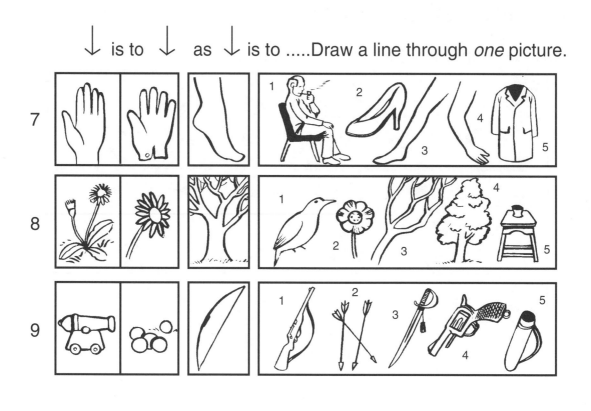

Draw a line through the picture which has something wrong with it.

Sort these pictures into the best order. Then draw a line through the first *and* last in the new order.

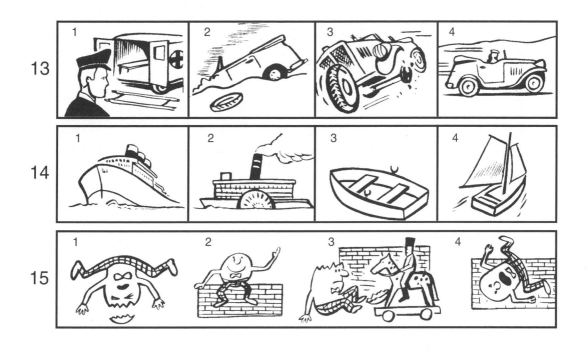

Draw a line through the picture which doesn't belong to the group.

Which one has something wrong? Draw a line through it.

Put these in a new order. Draw a line through the first and last.

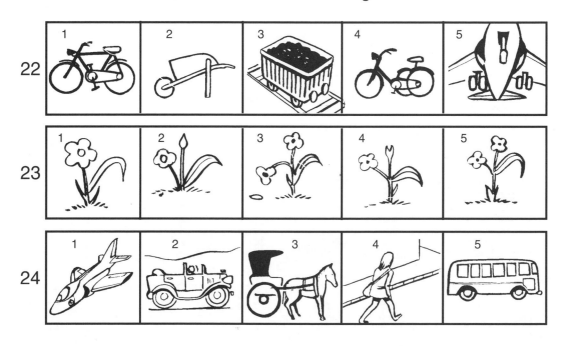

Score ..../24

B. Verbal Reasoning: Problems

James has three dogs, called Lex, Ben and Rover. One is white, one is black and one is brown.

The white dog is not called Lex. Lex is not brown. Rover is not brown.

1 So the brown dog is called ....

2 The white dog is called ....

3 The black dog is called ....

Here the words have been mixed up. Find their proper order and then write the answer to each question.

4 a has tails cat many how? ....

5 the what is coal of colour? ....

6 fishes legs have do? ....

7 how eyes many you have? ....

8 which Christmas month in is? ....

Helen has one sister, Natalie, and three brothers, David, Jack and Daniel.

9 How many children are there
in the family? (1 | 2 | 3 | 4 | 5 | 6)

10 How many brothers has Natalie? (0 | 1 | 2 | 3 | 4 | 5)

11 How many sisters has Natalie? (0 | 1 | 2 | 3 | 4 | 5)

12 How many sisters has Daniel? (0 | 1 | 2 | 3 | 4 | 5)

13 How many brothers has Jack? (0 | 1 | 2 | 3 | 4 | 5)

---

14 Which of the following words contains the sixth letter of the alphabet?

(horse | forest | cattle | bicycle | watch | puzzle)

15 Which one has legs, but cannot walk?

(a window | a dog | a worm | a horse | a chair)

16 If the day after tomorrow is Monday, which day of the week is today? ....

There are three women. One goes to work by car, one on a bicycle and one by bus.

Julia does not go by car.
The one who goes by bus is not Rachel.
Rachel does not go by car.
Jenny and Rachel are friends.

17 So the woman who goes by car is   ....

18 The woman who goes by bus is   ....

19 The woman who goes on a bicycle is   ....

Class	A	B	C	D	E
Girls	17	18	13	14	16
Boys	15	18	17	17	19
Total	32	36	30	31	35

A school has five classes, called A, B, C, D and E.

Class A has 17 girls and 15 boys and so on.

20 Which class has the largest number of boys?

(A | B | C | D | E)

21 Which class has the smallest number of girls?

(A | B | C | D | E)

22 Which class is the largest?   (A | B | C | D | E)

23 Which class has equal numbers of boys and girls?

(A | B | C | D | E)

---

24 If the day before yesterday was Tuesday, what day will it be
    tomorrow?   ....

25 Emma was born in 1985. She has a sister exactly 3 years
    older. In which year was her sister born?   ....

26 John is two years younger than William. William is eight years
    old. How old is John?   .... years

**In our village there are a doctor, a shopkeeper and a teacher.
Their surnames are Scott, Davis and Jones.**

**Scott knows nothing about medicine.
The doctor is not called Jones.
Jones is not the shopkeeper.**

27 So the doctor is called ....
28 The shopkeeper is called ....
29 The teacher is called ....

**Four boys stand in a line, one behind another. John is first,
Bill second, Henry third and Edward fourth. Edward and John
change places and Henry and Bill change places.**

30 Who is last in the line now?   (John I Bill I Henry I Edward)
31 Who is second in the line now?
                                      (John I Bill I Henry I Edward)
32 Who comes just in front of Henry now?
                                      (John I Bill I Edward I No one)

---

33 A certain class contains twice as many boys as girls. All the
    boys have dark hair, but only half of the girls have dark hair.
    Five girls have fair hair. How many pupils are there in the
    class?   .... pupils

34 I am going on holiday in 11 weeks' time. If today is April 29th, in
    which *month* do I go on holiday?   ....

A, B, C, D and E are five girls.
A and E are tall; the others are short.
C, D and E swim; the others do not swim.
A and C play tennis but not golf; the others play golf.

35 Which of the tall girls swims? ....

36 Which girl plays tennis and swims? ....

37 Which of the tall girls plays tennis? ....

38 Which of the short girls does not swim? ....

39 Which *two* girls play golf and swim? .... and ....

---

40 Which of the following has both wings and claws?
　　　　(cat | lobster | butterfly | parrot | lion | aeroplane)
41 Which of the following has legs and eyes but no teeth?
　　　　(horse | dog | snake | bird | rabbit | shark)
42 Which of the following lives on land but has no legs?
　　　　(beetle | tortoise | snail | ant | fish | bird)

Day	A	B	C	D	E
Sunrise (a.m.)	3.45	3.43	3.43	3.45	3.50
Sunset (p.m.)	8.14	8.18	8.21	8.21	8.18

The table shows the time at which the sun rose and set on each of five days, lettered A to E.

43 On which day was the earliest sunset? (A | B | C | D | E)
44 On how many of the days did the sun rise before 3.45 a.m.?
　　　　　　　　　　　　(1 | 2 | 3 | 4 | 5)
45 On how many of the days did the sun set before 8.20 p.m.?
　　　　　　　　　　　　(1 | 2 | 3 | 4 | 5)
46 Which was the longest day?　　　(A | B | C | D | E)
47 Which was the shortest day?　　　(A | B | C | D | E)

A, B, C, D, E and F are six cargo boats.
Only A, B and C carry meat.
Only A, D and F carry butter.
Only B, E and F carry fruit.

48 Which boat carries both butter and fruit?
(A | B | C | D | E | F)

49 Which boat carries both meat and fruit?
(A | B | C | D | E | F)

50 Which boat carries both meat and butter?
(A | B | C | D | E | F)

51 Which boat carries neither meat nor fruit?
(A | B | C | D | E | F)

---

52 Straight lines are drawn joining a point inside a square to each of the four corners. Into how many parts is the square divided?
(1 | 2 | 4 | 5 | 8 | 12)

53 Peter is John's father, so John is Peter's
(brother | grandfather | son | uncle | father).

54 Diana is Jim's sister and Jim is Tom's brother, so Diana is Tom's   (cousin | sister | aunt | daughter | mother).

Gary had a white mouse. He exchanged this mouse with Kate for a canary, which Kate had obtained from Sam in return for a rabbit. Sam had obtained this canary from George.

55 Who had the canary first of all? ....

56 Who now has the canary? ....

57 Who now has the rabbit? ....

58 If at the end Kate exchanges with George, what will Kate have then? ....

Anne is shorter than Isabel but taller than Tom, while Peter is taller than Isabel but shorter than Rebecca.

59 Who is the tallest but one?

(Anne | Rebecca | Isabel | Tom | Peter)

60 Who is the shortest?

(Anne | Rebecca | Isabel | Tom | Peter)

61 Who is the shortest but one?

(Anne | Rebecca | Isabel | Tom | Peter)

Crop	1983	1984	1985	1986	1987	1988
Wheat	97	91	96	92	94	89
Potatoes	96	90	84	94	95	96

The table shows how good the harvests of two crops were in each of six years: the higher the figure, the better the harvest.

62 Which year was the best for wheat?

(1983 | 1984 | 1985 | 1986 | 1987 | 1988)

63 How many years separate the harvesting of the worst two potato crops?

(0 | 1 | 2 | 3 | 4 | 5)

64 When did the wheat harvest appear to be most different from the potato crop?

(1983 | 1984 | 1985 | 1986 | 1987 | 1988)

65 When was the rise in the potato harvest greatest from one year to the next? Mark *both* years.

(1983 | 1984 | 1985 | 1986 | 1987 | 1988)

Score ..../65

12

C. Verbal Reasoning: Symbols

A B C D E F G H I J K L M N O P Q R S T U V W X Y Z

1 Which letter comes midway between D and L in the alphabet?

....

2 Which letter in this set comes nearest the end of the alphabet?
E L B T W S N I   ....

3 Write these four letters in the order they come in the alphabet:
S O U R   ....

4 Two letters in this set come next to one another in the alphabet.
Write them *both*: W U N K C T I
.... and ....

Underline the one word in each group which *cannot* be made from the word in capitals.

***Example*:** TON   not │ no │ **too** │ on │ to

The word *too* is underlined because it cannot be made from TON: 'T' and 'O' are there, but not a second 'O'.

5 CRAM   car │ race │ mar │ arm │ arc
6 CREAM   cram │ mare │ crane │ race │ care
7 SPITE   tips │ pies │ step │ spies │ pets
8 GLOWS   slow │ logs │ lows │ slog │ goals

A stands for 4, B stands for 1, C stands for 3 and D stands for 2. So instead of writing 21, we write DB and instead of 1 + 2 = 3, we put B + D = C. The answer to the sum "A − C" is B because 4 − 3 = 1.

9 Write 312 in letters.   ....

10 Write ACD in figures.   ....

11 Add C and D, then take away A.
What *letter* is the answer?   ....

12 What letter is twice as big as D?   ....

13

A B C D E F G H I J K L M N O P Q R S T U V W X Y Z

13 If the letters B, E and F were not in the alphabet,
the first four letters would be: ....

14 Which letter in this set comes nearest the end of
the alphabet? D U N H R K P ....

15 Write the letter that comes most often in this set of letters:
C L X M C P L L C P C ....

16 Two letters in this set come next to one another in the alphabet.
Write them *both*:

B H O L G Y V .... and ....

Underline the one word which *cannot* be made from the word in capitals.

17	WEST	stew	stem	sew	wet	set
18	TEAM	mate	meat	tame	ate	meet
19	TRAIN	trim	rant	tarn	rain	tar
20	GREAT	grate	agree	rage	gate	tear
21	SLOW	lows	owl	slew	sow	owls
22	LEAP	peel	pale	pal	peal	ale
23	RIDES	side	reside	dries	sire	side

24 If BZAE stands for 'dolt', then AZE stands for
(lot | lob | toll | doll | old).

25 If DIFP stands for 'brag', then PIFD stands for
(age | rag | garb | grab | bar).

26 If MICD stands for 'rose', then IMD stands for
(roe | oar | ore | sore | era).

27 If WUBL stands for 'seat', then LUB stands for
(ate | east | sat | tea | set).

28 If VFOG stands for 'snap', then GOFV stands for
(pans | naps | span | amps | maps).

A B C D E F G H I J K L M N O P Q R S T U V W X Y Z

29 If there are more than 5 letters between G and N
    write O, if not P.   ....

30 If the letters U, X and Z were not in the alphabet,
    the last four letters would be: ....

31 Count how many different letters there are in
    this set: E H L H E N E H N J.
    Write the *number*.   ....

32 Which letter comes only twice in the set below?
    V X W V L K W X K K L X X W V   ....

Find the rule for each row and then write the letter or set of letters that should come *next*.

Example:	A	C	E	G	....
33	B	E	H	K	....
34	L	J	H	F	....
35	Y	V	S	P	....
36	BC	CD	DE	EF	....
37	BD	EG	HJ	KM	....

38 If BROG stands for 'lamp', then ORG stands for
                        (pal l lap l amp l alp l map).

39 If BONT stands for 'pear', then NBO stands for
                        (ape l pea l are l rap l ear).

40 If YLWS stands for 'coat', then WYS stands for
                        (cat l act l oat l oak l coo).

41 If UGHE stands for 'glow', then HEG stands for
                        (low l log l owl l goal l go).

42 If HIMC stands for 'play', then CMH stands for
                        (pal l alp l yap l pay l lay).

In each question, find the rule by which the second word in each pair has been made out of the first and then complete the third pair.

Example: bin, in;   bone, one;   bat, ...<u>at</u>........

43   cart, cat; pint, pit;   seat, ...

44   nip, pin;   saw, was;   rat, ...

45   slap, pal; draw, war;   fees, ...

46   last, loot; mend, mood;   pull, ...

---

47 Which two letters occur least often in the word DISINTERESTED?   .... and ....

48 Write the fourth letter of the third month of the year. ....

49 Which letter occurs in the words SEPTEMBER and APRIL but not in the word COUNTRY?   ....

In a code A stands for 3, B for 8, C for 10, D for 12, E for 20, F for 30 and G for 48. Underline your answer to each of these questions.

50 B years ago Kay was D years old. How old is she now?

                  (A | B | C | D | E | F | G) years

51 D parcels have arrived, but E were due. How many have still to arrive?   (A | B | C | D | E | F | G) parcels

52 How many hours are there from C a.m. to C p.m.?

                  (A | B | C | D | E | F | G) hours

53 C hours from now it will be B p.m. What is the time now?

                  (A | B | C | D | E | F | G) a.m.

Here are four words: PAD   SOP   SAD   POD

Below, the same words are put in a different order in code. The code is the same all through. Find the right word for each code:

54 δ β μ ....   56 μ β π ....

55 δ λ π ....   57 μ λ π ....

In each question, underline one word which *cannot* be made by rearranging all or some of the letters in the word MECHANISATION.

58	those	chosen	shine	stance	chew
59	machine	change	teams	noise	chant
60	shame	mast	mention	miser	teach
61	moths	anthem	scheme	mascot	nation

A B C D E F G H I J K L M N O P Q R S T U V W X Y Z

Find the rule for each row and then write the letter or set of letters that should come *next*:

62	C	F	I	L	....
63	AZ	CY	EX	GW	....
64	ZA	XC	VE	TG	....
65	ST	PQ	MN	JK	....
66	MN	LO	KP	JQ	....

In a certain code the word GET is written as COL and the word HOLD is written as APIN. Write the *code* word for each of these:

67 THE ....

68 DOLT ....

69 HEDGE ....

The next three words are written in the same code. Write the meaning of each word:

70 CPL ....

71 AOIN ....

72 IPNCO ....

Here are five words:

LEAN   REAL   EARN   NEAR   LANE

Below, the same words are put in code but in a different order. Find the right word for each code.

73   △   +   ○   □   ....

74   △   □   +   ○   ....

75   □   +   ×   ○   ....

76   ○   □   +   ×   ....

77   ×   □   +   △   ....

---

78   In a certain code the word DAB is written as BAD and the word PART is written as TRAP. How would the word GNAT be written?   ....

79   In another code the word RING is written as GRIN and the word LEAP is written as PLEA. How would the word HINT be written?   ....

80   In yet another code the word SIFT is written as FITS and the word EAST is written as SATE. How would the word MOPE be written?   ....

Score ..../80

D. Verbal Reasoning: Concepts

Example: Look in the brackets for a word that goes with 'cat' just as 'puppy' goes with 'dog'. The word is 'kitten': underline 'kitten'.

dog – puppy .... cat – (fur | play | <u>kitten</u> | young | milk)

Now do these.
1 grass – green ..... snow – (winter | cold | white | storm | flakes)
2 car – driver .... plane – (pilot | air | fly | hostess | wings)
3 three – third ..... four – (half | eight | one | fourth | second)
4 end – stop ..... beginning – (start | try | time | now | first)

What is the best ending? Underline it.
5 A party always has
(ice-cream | paper hats | jelly | fancy-dress | people).
6 A garden always has
(trees | earth | a lawn | a gate | hedges).
7 A school always has
(pupils | a hall | a headmaster | boys | girls).

Think of the best order to put the things in, then mark the first _and_ the last in the new order.

Example: pig | <u>elephant</u> | sparrow | <u>fly</u> | horse

8   7 | 1 | 9 | 5 | 3
9   tiny | big | huge | small
10   third | fourth | sixth | fifth | second
11   March | July | June | May | April

Which one doesn't belong with the others? Underline it.

12 groan | moan | wail | sing | weep

13 scowling | laughing | happy | cheerful | smiling

14 aunt | uncle | grandfather | niece | nephew

15 coat | hair | gloves | trousers | hat

Think of the best order to put things in, then underline the first _and_ the last in the new order.

16 codfish | whale | shark | goldfish

17 month | week | day | year | fortnight

18 puddle | pond | ocean | lake

19 CD | EF | AB | DE | BC

In each question, look at the first example of a word-pair; underline the best word to make a similar pair.

20 glove – hand ..... shoe – (leather | sole | horse | toes | foot)

21 pillow – bed ..... cushion – (square | chair | soft | feathers | silk)

22 Rome – Italy ..... Paris –
      (French | France | Berlin | capital | Europe)

23 bite – teeth ..... scratch – (hurt | claws | knife | pin | pain)

Underline the best ending for each sentence.

24 A box always has (straw | sides | contents | a lid | wood).

25 A meal always has (food | soup | bread | meat | sauce).

26 A tree always has
      (leaves | a trunk | fruit | berries | nests | blossom).

27 A river always has
      (trees | rocks | a waterfall | water | a bridge).

Which one doesn't belong? Underline it.

28 elf | fairy | goblin | shepherd | pixie

29 saw | axe | knife | scissors | tongs

30 run | step | write | hop | walk

31 hail | sleet | rain | wind | snow

Underline the best word to make a similar pair.

32 boy – son ..... girl – (sonny | twin | sister | daughter | mother)

33 grass – field ..... water – (lake | tap | drink | cold | swim)

34 water – swim ..... ice – (skate | cream | hot | winter | axe)

35 tiny – small ..... huge – (minute | big | little | mass | more)

Underline the best ending.

36 A teapot always has

(a kettle | tea | a cosy | water | a spout | a cup).

37 An island always has

(trees | a boat | cliffs | people | mountains | a shore).

38 An coat always has

(a coat-hanger | pockets | a velvet collar | armholes | a belt).

Which one doesn't belong? Underline it.

39 quilt | blanket | sheet | eiderdown | tablecloth

40 calf | foal | kitten | lamb | horse

41 dull | murky | dismal | stupid | cloudy

42 lock | fix | return | tie | fasten

43 empty | clear | deserted | bare | quiet

In the brackets there is *one* word which is like the three words in capitals but different from all the others. Underline it.

Example: PLUM, PEAR, ORANGE

(lettuce | wheat | grass | <u>apple</u> | onion)

44 WIPE, MOP, SCRUB

(serve | wave | finish | mark | sponge)

45 WHISPER, BABBLE, GURGLE

(murmur | shriek | clatter | bawl | sniff)

46 PAINT, GILD, ENAMEL

(draw | cover | write | scrub | varnish)

47 KNAVE, VILLAIN, ROGUE

(raven | rascal | tramp | savage | beggar)

48 APE, BABOON, GORILLA

(squirrel | zoo | animal | jungle | monkey)

Make similar pairs of words.

49 me – mine .... he – (him | her | she | his | thine)

50 bed – lie ..... chair – (table | sit | cushion | sleep | lift)

51 go – come .... buy – (goods | send | pay | sell | shop)

52 sparrow – beak ..... pig – (sty | snout | hide | pork | trotter)

Underline the one word which is *different* from the rest.

53 picture | drawing | painting | frame | photograph | portrait

54 tree | bush | earth | grass | vegetable | flower

55 decide | search | investigate | examine | seek

56 trawler | cruiser | submarine | battleship | liner | cargo-boat

---

Think of the best order, then mark the first _and_ last in the new order.

57	youth	|	baby	|	toddler	|	adult	| schoolgirl

57   youth \| baby \| toddler \| adult \| schoolgirl

58   mansion \| palace \| house \| hut \| cottage

59   city \| room \| house \| village \| town

60   o \| u \| e \| i \| a

Which word is like the three in capitals but different from all the others?

61   NEEDLE, THORN, TACK
       (thread \| spike \| sew \| saw \| sharp)

62   HANDCUFFED, MUZZLED, SHACKLED
       (punished \| cruel \| afraid \| bridled \| sad)

63   KINGDOM, COUNTRY, DOMINION
       (place \| crown \| state \| royal \| capital)

64   MYTH, LEGEND, TALE
       (song \| fairy \| fable \| false \| book)

65   CALM, STILL, PEACEFUL
       (closed \| disturbed \| summer \| story \| unruffled)

66   AGITATED, DISTURBED, TROUBLED
       (cramped \| dizzy \| weak \| shaken \| calm)

Underline the word which means _either_ nearly the same as or nearly the opposite of the word in capitals.

67   ODD   (seven \| many \| number \| unusual \| four \| known)

68   TREMBLE   (jump \| voice \| fear \| stamp \| shiver \| frighten)

69   COLLECT   (select \| accept \| fare \| scatter \| money \| right)

70   SLENDER   (quick \| receiver \| tender \| stumble \| slime \| thick)

71   LEAD   (sink \| follow \| guard \| heavy \| officer \| dog)

Write one letter for each cross.

Example: FINGER is to H........*and*........ as T........*oe*........ is to FOOT.
x x x   x x

72 SPEAKER is to S........................ as S........................ is to SING.
                 x x x x   x x x x x

73 CUFF is to S........................ as H........................ is to ARM.
           x x x x   x x x

74 CATTLE is to L........................ as S........................ is to BLEAT.
             x x   x x x x

75 CLIMBER is to C........................ as S........................ is to SWIM.
              x x x x   x x x x x

76 NOBODY is to N........................ as S........................ is to SOMETHING.
             x x x x x   x x x x x x

The words in each of the groups A to E are alike in some way but different from the words in the other groups.

A	B	C	D	E
wood	store	mill	tool	harbour
coal	pantry	workshop	engine	jetty
cement	depot	pottery	wheel	wharf

Find which is the correct group for each of the words below and write the group letter beside the word.

Example: timber ......**A**...... larder ......**B**......

77 machine ....   82 metal ....

78 quay ....   83 factory ....

79 crafts ....   84 clay ....

80 lever ....   85 barn ....

81 cellar ....

Score ..../85

E. Non-verbal Reasoning

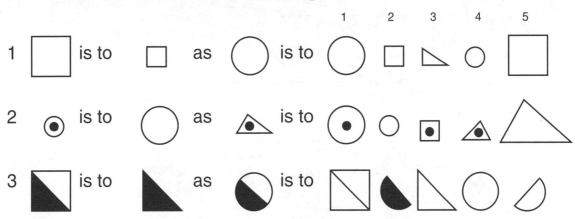

1 ☐ is to ☐ as ◯ is to

2 ⊙ is to ◯ as ◬ is to

3 ◨ is to ◣ as ◐ is to

How many little squares like Ⓐ make up each shape?

Example:

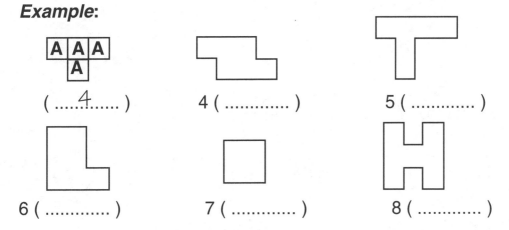

(....4....)

4 (............)

5 (............)

6 (............)

7 (............)

8 (............)

Which one doesn't belong?

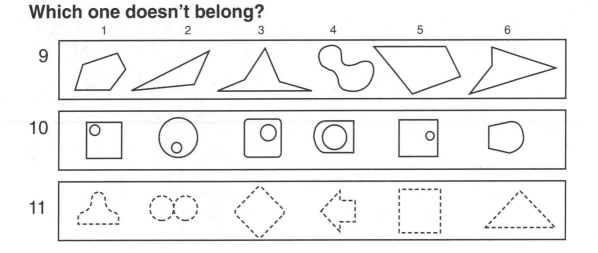

Put these into a new order and mark the first and last.

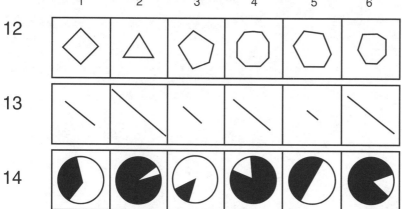

12

13

14

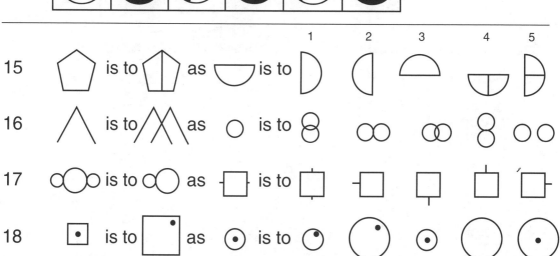

15   ⬠ is to ⬠ as ◡ is to   1   2   3   4   5

16   ∧ is to ∧∧ as ○ is to

17   ○○ is to ○○ as ⊣▢ is to

18   ▣ is to ▢ as ◉ is to

Which drawing is needed to complete each pattern?

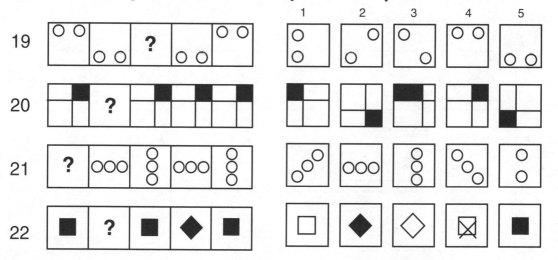

19

20

21

22

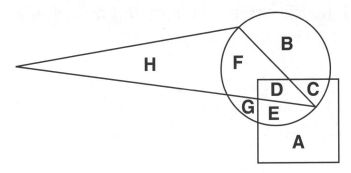

23 Which letter is in the square, but not in the circle or the triangle? ....

24 Which letter is in the circle and the triangle, but not in the square? ....

25 Which letter is in the circle and the triangle and the square? ....

26 Which *two* letters are in the circle, but not in the square or the triangle? .... and ....

Put these into a new order and mark the first and last.

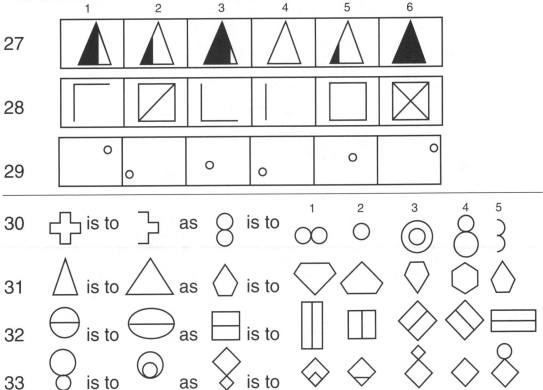

27

28

29

30

31

32

33

Which one looks the same, but is facing the other way?

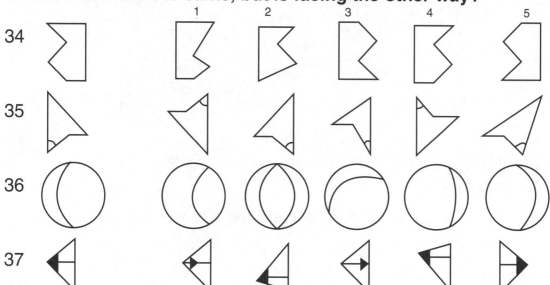

34

35

36

37

Write the missing number.

38   9, 8, 7, 6, ...

39   1, 4, 7, 10, ...

40   13, 11, 9, 7, ...

41   16, 8, 4, 2, ...

42   23, 29, 35, 41, ...

43   35, 30, ... , 20, 15

44   5, 14, 23, ... , 41

45   0, 1, 3, 6, ...

Put these into a new order and mark the first and last.

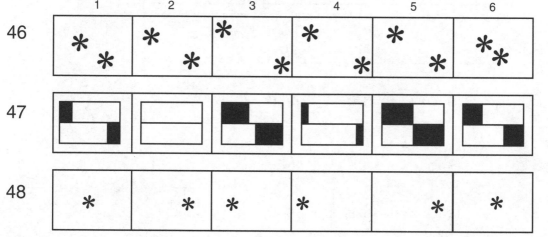

46

47

48

How many little squares like A make up each shape?

Example:

 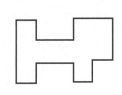 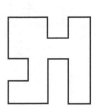 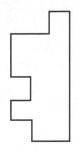 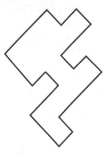

(......4......)   49 (..........) 50 (..........) 51 (.........) 52 (..........)

Which drawing is needed to complete each pattern?

53
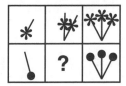

1	2	3	4	5

54

1	2	3	4	5

55

1	2	3	4	5

Write the missing number.

56   64, ... , 16, 8, 4, 2

57   2, 5, 9, 14, 20, ...

58   6, 8½, 11, 13½, ...

59   42, 35, 28, 21, ...

60   ½, ¼, ⅛, 1/16, ...

Which drawing is needed to complete each pattern?

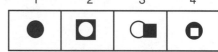

61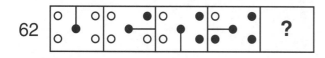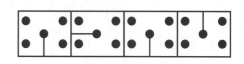

62

63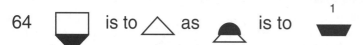

64  is to as is to

65 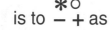 is to as is to

66 + −
　 ○ ✳ is to ✳ ○
　 　　 − + as ○ □
　　　　　　　 ■ ● is to ○ □　●■　□○　■●　□●
　　　　　　　　　　　　　 ■●　□○　●■　○□　○■

Which one looks the same, but is facing the other way?

67

68

69

70

Score ..../70

30

Answers

Pages 3–6. A. Picture Reasoning

1. 3	2. 6	3. 3	4. 2	5. 2	6. 5
7. 2	8. 3	9. 2	10. 1	11. 5	12. 5
13. 4/1	14. 3/1	15. 2/3	16. 1	17. 4	18. 5
19. 2	20. 5	21. 4	22. 2/5	23. 1/3	24. 4/1

Pages 7–12. B. Verbal Reasoning: Problems

1. Ben	2. Rover	3. Lex	4. one	5. black
6. no	7. two	8. December	9. five	10. three
11. one	12. two	13. two	14. forest	15. a chair
16. Saturday	17. Jenny	18. Julia	19. Rachel	20. E
21. C	22. B	23. B	24. Friday	25. 1982
26. six	27. Davis	28. Scott	29. Jones	30. John
31. Henry	32. Edward	33. 30	34. July	35. E
36. C	37. A	38. B	39. D and E	40. parrot
41. bird	42. snail	43. A	44. two	45. three
46. C	47. E	48. F	49. B	50. A
51. D	52. four	53. son	54. sister	55. George
56. Gary	57. Sam	58. nothing	59. Peter	60. Tom
61. Anne	62. 1983	63. one	64. 1985	65. 1985/1986

Pages 13–18. C. Verbal Reasoning: Symbols

1. H	2. W	3. ORSU	4. T and U	5. race
6. crane	7. spies	8. goals	9. CBD	10. 432
11. B	12. A	13. ACDG	14. U	15. C
16. G and H	17. stem	18. meet	19. trim	20. agree
21. slew	22. peel	23. reside	24. lot	25. grab
26. ore	27. tea	28. pans	29. O	30. TVWY
31. five	32. L	33. N	34. D	35. M
36. FG	37. NP	38. map	39. ape	40. act
41. owl	42. yap	43. set	44. tar	45. see
46. pool	47. N and R	48. C	49. P	50. E
51. B	52. D	53. C	54. SOP	55. SAD
56. POD	57. PAD	58. chew	59. change	60. miser
61. scheme	62. O	63. IV	64. RI	65. GH
66. IR	67. LAO	68. NPIL	69. AONCO	70. GOT
71. HELD	72. LODGE	73. LANE	74. LEAN	75. EARN
76. NEAR	77. REAL	78. TANG	79. THIN	80. POEM

Pages 19–24. D. Verbal Reasoning: Concepts

1. white	2. pilot	3. fourth	4. start	5. people
6. earth	7. pupils	8. 1/9	9. tiny/huge	10. second/sixth
11. March, July	12. sing	13. scowling	14. grandfather	15. hair
16. goldfish/ whale	17. day/year	18. puddle/ocean	19. AB/EF	20. foot
21. chair	22. France	23. claws	24. sides	25. food
26. a trunk	27. water	28. shepherd	29. tongs	30. write
31. wind	32. daughter	33. lake	34. skate	35. big
36. a spout	37. a shore	38. armholes	39. tablecloth	40. horse
41. stupid	42. return	43. quiet	44. sponge	45. murmur
46. varnish	47. rascal	48. monkey	49. his	50. sit
51. sell	52. snout	53. frame	54. earth	55. decide
56. submarine	57. baby/adult	58. hut/palace	59. room/city	60. a/u
61. spike	62. bridled	63. state	64. fable	65. unruffled
66. shaken	67. unusual	68. shiver	69. scatter	70. thick
71. follow	72. SPEAK, SINGER	73. SLEEVE, HAND	74. LOW, SHEEP	75. CLIMB, SWIMMER
76. NOTHING, SOMEBODY	77. D	78. E	79. C	80. D
81. B	82. A	83. C	84. A	85. B

Pages 25–30. E. Non-verbal Reasoning

1. four	2. five	3. two	4. six	5. six	6. seven
7. four	8. seven	9. four	10. six	11. two	12. two/four
13. five/two	14. two/three	15. four	16. three	17. two	18. two
19. four	20. four	21. three	22. two	23. A	24. F
25. D	26. B and G	27. four/six	28. four/six	29. two/six	30. five
31. two	32. five	33. one	34. four	35. two	36. five
37. five	38. five	39. 13	40. five	41. one	42. 47
43. 25	44. 32	45. 10	46. six/three	47. two/five	48. four/five
49. 10	50. 12	51. 14	52. 13	53. two	54. five
55. one	56. 32	57. 27	58. 16	59. 14	60. $1/32$
61. two	62. four	63. one	64. one	65. two	66. two
67. three	68. three	69. two	70. one		

Mental Arithmetic

AGE 9-11

Dr Bill Gillham

As a parent, you can play an important part in your child's education by your interest and encouragement. This book is designed to help you develop your child's ability in mental arithmetic. It will:

- help them to *understand* what goes on in arithmetic.
- help them to see that calculators can't do your thinking for you.
- make them more mentally agile. (You become intelligent by *using* your brain.)
- help them to avoid calculator mistakes because they will know roughly what the answer to a calculation should be. *Guess-estimating is as important as being exactly right.*
- help them to use arithmetic in practical, real-life situations.
- help them to become fluent in the four rules of arithmetic: addition, subtraction, multiplication and division.

The book is divided into seven sections, each containing four tests, the fourth of which is a check test. Finally there is an end-of-book test and a rating chart to show how well your child has done.

*Hodder
Children's
Books*

NCPTA

The only home learning programme supported by the NCPTA

How to help your child

- Don't expect them to do more than one test a day.

- Make sure they can read the words in the questions before they try to answer them.

- Explain that they must not work things out on paper – it has to be done in their heads!

- If they can't do a question after they've thought about it tell them to put a ? against it and to go on to the next one.

- The check test should be an oral test. Read the questions out loud for your child to answer without looking at the book.

- Mark the tests, being careful to use the 'nearly right' category.

- Go over mistakes by talking them through, not working them out on paper.

- Give plenty of praise. Children thrive on success!

> 1 kilogramme (kg) = 1000 grammes (g)
> 1 kilometre (km) = 1000 metres (m)
> 1 metre (m) = 100 centimetres (cm)
> 1 centimetre (cm) = 10 millimetres (mm)

The right of Dr Bill Gillham to be identified
as the author of the Work has been asserted by him in
accordance with the Copyright, Designs and Patents Act 1988.

Published by Hodder Children's Books 1995

Copyright © WEC Gillham 1983

Printed and bound in Great Britain

Hodder Children's Books
A division of Hodder Headline
338 Euston Road
London NW1 3BH

Previously published as Test Your Child's Mental Arithmetic

The answer goes in the box

1A

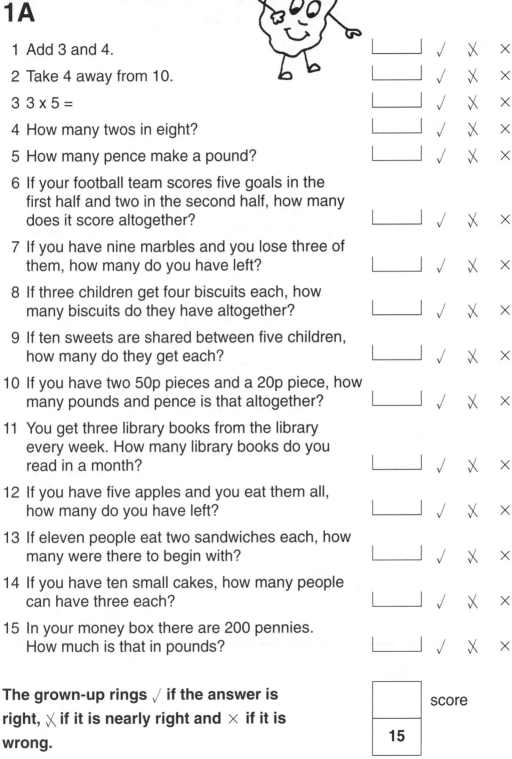

1 Add 3 and 4.

2 Take 4 away from 10.

3 3 x 5 =

4 How many twos in eight?

5 How many pence make a pound?

6 If your football team scores five goals in the first half and two in the second half, how many does it score altogether?

7 If you have nine marbles and you lose three of them, how many do you have left?

8 If three children get four biscuits each, how many biscuits do they have altogether?

9 If ten sweets are shared between five children, how many do they get each?

10 If you have two 50p pieces and a 20p piece, how many pounds and pence is that altogether?

11 You get three library books from the library every week. How many library books do you read in a month?

12 If you have five apples and you eat them all, how many do you have left?

13 If eleven people eat two sandwiches each, how many were there to begin with?

14 If you have ten small cakes, how many people can have three each?

15 In your money box there are 200 pennies. How much is that in pounds?

The grown-up rings √ if the answer is right, ⅄ if it is nearly right and ✕ if it is wrong.

score

15

3

No working out on paper

1B

1 Add 5 and 3.

2 Take 5 away from 11.

3 4 x 4 =

4 How many threes in nine?

5 What is half of ten?

6 What is 235p in pounds and pence?

7 If there are five chairs in one room, two in another and six in another, how many are there altogether?

8 If twelve children are invited to a party and three can't come, how many come to the party?

9 If there are six boxes with three pencils in each, how many pencils are there altogether?

10 If a caterpillar has twenty feet, how many pairs of shoes will he need?

11 If your teacher has sixteen pencils and half of them get broken, how many are left?

12 You have two 20p pieces and one 10p piece. How much more do you need to make a pound?

13 If four stamps of the same value cost £1, how much did they cost each?

14 If you have fifteen marbles, buy four more and then lose two, how many are you left with?

15 In a class of 24 children there are only six rubbers. How many children have to share one rubber?

Write down the answer only

score

15

4

Work it out in your head
1C

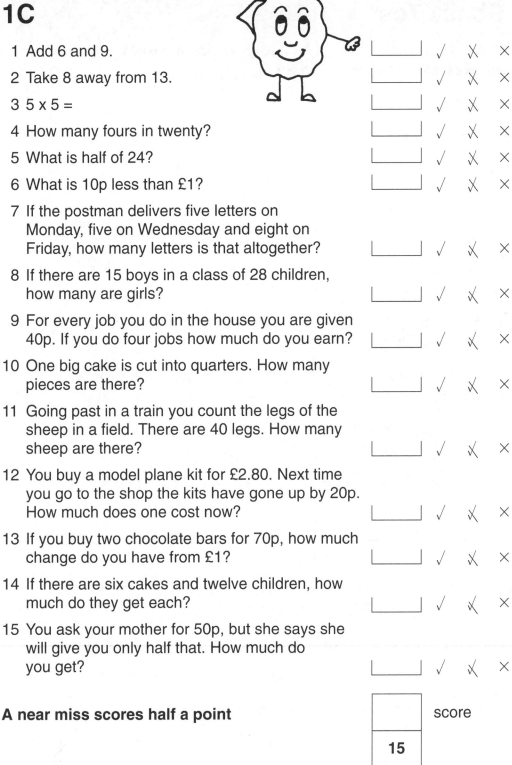

1 Add 6 and 9.

2 Take 8 away from 13.

3 5 x 5 =

4 How many fours in twenty?

5 What is half of 24?

6 What is 10p less than £1?

7 If the postman delivers five letters on Monday, five on Wednesday and eight on Friday, how many letters is that altogether?

8 If there are 15 boys in a class of 28 children, how many are girls?

9 For every job you do in the house you are given 40p. If you do four jobs how much do you earn?

10 One big cake is cut into quarters. How many pieces are there?

11 Going past in a train you count the legs of the sheep in a field. There are 40 legs. How many sheep are there?

12 You buy a model plane kit for £2.80. Next time you go to the shop the kits have gone up by 20p. How much does one cost now?

13 If you buy two chocolate bars for 70p, how much change do you have from £1?

14 If there are six cakes and twelve children, how much do they get each?

15 You ask your mother for 50p, but she says she will give you only half that. How much do you get?

A near miss scores half a point

score

15

5

The check test is an oral test

1D Check Test

The adult asks the questions, the child gives the answers.
Any mistakes should be followed up.

1 Add 6 and 9.

2 Take 5 away from 11.

3 4 x 4 =

4 How many twos in eight?

5 What is half of 24?

6 If your football team scores five goals in the first half and two in the second half, how many does it score altogether?

7 If there are five chairs in one room, two in another and six in another, how many are there altogether?

8 If three children get four biscuits each, how many biscuits do they have altogether?

9 For every job you do in the house you are given 40p. If you do four jobs how much do you earn?

10 If you have two 50p pieces and a 20p piece, how many pounds and pence is that altogether?

11 If your teacher has sixteen pencils and half of them get broken, how many are left?

12 You buy a model plane kit for £2.80. Next time you go to the shop the kits have gone up by 20p. How much does one cost now?

13 If four stamps of the same value cost £1, how much did they cost each?

14 If you have ten small cakes, how many people can have three each?

15 You ask your mother for 50p, but she says she will give you only half that. How much do you get?

No pencil needed for the check test

A good guess is better than nothing

2A

GUESS!

1 Add 6 and 3 and 4. ☐ ✓ ✗ ✗

2 Take 8 away from 17. ☐ ✓ ✗ ✗

3 4 x 6 = ☐ ✓ ✗ ✗

4 How many sevens in twenty-one? ☐ ✓ ✗ ✗

5 What is quarter of forty? ☐ ✓ ✗ ✗

6 What is 15p more than 90p? ☐ ✓ ✗ ✗

7 Shooting a rifle at the funfair you score
six, two, a miss and three. What is your
total score? ☐ ✓ ✗ ✗

8 If you get $^7/_{10}$, $^8/_{10}$ and $^5/_{10}$ in three spelling tests,
how many spellings did you get wrong altogether? ☐ ✓ ✗ ✗

9 With each packet of cornflakes there is a 10p
token. How much do you have in tokens from
five packets? ☐ ✓ ✗ ✗

10 You have twelve sweets but you give a quarter
of them to your sister. How many does she get? ☐ ✓ ✗ ✗

11 On craft afternoon your teacher asks you to
give out 3 paint pots to each child in the class
who is doing painting. You give out 18 pots.
How many children are doing painting? ☐ ✓ ✗ ✗

12 What is 50p less than £1.25? ☐ ✓ ✗ ✗

13 If you buy three sticks of bubble-gum at 10p
each, how much change do you have from 50p? ☐ ✓ ✗ ✗

14 If there are three cakes and twelve children,
how much do they get each? ☐ ✓ ✗ ✗

15 When you go to the library you expect the fine
on your book to be 25p but it costs three times
as much. How much does it cost? ☐ ✓ ✗ ✗

Read the questions carefully

☐ score

15

7

Don't use your fingers – use your head

2B

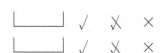

1 Add 5 and 6 and 7.

2 Take 6 away from 15.

3 4 x 7 =

4 How many sixes in thirty-six?

5 What is a quarter of twenty-four?

6 What is 20p less than £1.10?

7 Playing cricket you score a six and two fours before being clean bowled. What is your total score?

8 You buy a model plane kit which should have 24 parts, but 5 are missing. How many pieces are you left with?

9 You are saving 5p pieces in a tin. When you count them you have eighteen. How much is that altogether?

10 It is Bonfire Night and you have let off half your fireworks. You have nine left. How many did you start with?

11 You have 25 sheets of paper and you have to give out 3 to each child in your class. If you have one left over how many children have you given paper to?

12 If you have a quarter of an hour for playtime, how many minutes is that?

13 If you buy two comics that cost the same and you have 20p change from £1, how much did the comics cost *each*?

14 Your mother gives you six chocolate biscuits to share with your brother. If you eat twice as many as he does, how many does he get?

15 You get $^{10}/_{20}$ in a maths test but the boy next to you in class gets half as much again. What is his mark?

Use your pencil only for writing the answer

score

15

Keep your brain dusted!

2C

1 Add 3 and 0 and 9.

2 Take 8 away from 13.

3 8 x 2 =

4 How many fours in forty-eight?

5 What is half of forty-four?

6 What is 30p less than £1.20?

7 You have seven pieces of red Lego and four pieces of blue Lego. Your friend gives you five more pieces of red Lego and six more pieces of blue Lego. How much do you have of the two colours now? (Give two answers please)

8 You have bought a giant set of 30 felt-tip pens. You lose three at school and lend four to a friend. How many do you have left?

9 When you ask your mother for some money, she gives you all the coins in her purse. There are four 20p pieces and four 5p pieces. How much do you get?

10 If you have an hour for lunch at school and it takes you 10 minutes to eat your dinner, how long do you have to play?

11 At a party you play a game where you are blindfolded, given a pack of 36 cards and told to walk round a circle of children giving one card to each child. When you have gone round the circle three times there are no cards left. How many children were there?

12 What is 21p more than £1.80?

13 You buy three rockets for Bonfire Night. From a five pound note you get a 20p piece, two 10p pieces, and two 5p pieces in change. How much did the rockets cost each?

14 If six children get half a chocolate bar each and two children get a whole one each, how many chocolate bars were there to start with?

15 If you are ten years old and your mother is three times as old as you, how old is she?

Write down the answer only

score

15

9

The check test is an oral test

2D Check Test

ORAL TEST

The adult asks the questions, the child gives the answers.
Any mistakes should be followed up.

1 Add 3 and 0 and 9.

2 Take 6 away from 15.

3 4 x 7 =

15 4 How many sevens in twenty-one? 3

5 What is half of forty-four?

14 6 What is 15p more than 90p?   £1.05

7 Playing cricket you score a six and two fours before being clean bowled. What is your total score?

8 If you get $^7/_{10}$, $^8/_{10}$ and $^5/_{10}$ in three spelling tests, how many spellings did you get wrong altogether?

9 When you ask your mother for some money she gives you all the coins in her purse. There are four 20p pieces and four 5p pieces. How much do you get?

10 You have twelve sweets but you give a quarter of them to your sister. How many does she get?

11 You have 25 sheets of paper and you have to give out 3 to each child in your class. If you have one left over how many children have you given paper to?

12 What is 21p more than £1.80?

13 If you buy two comics that cost the same and you have 20p change from £1, how much did the comics cost *each*?

14 If there are three cakes and twelve children, how much do they get each?

15 If you are ten years old and your mother is three times as old as you, how old is she?

No pencil needed for the check test

Your brain is the best calculator – it needs no batteries!

3A

1 Add 1 and 2 and 3 and 4. ☐ ✓ X ✗

2 Take 6 away from 11. ☐ ✓ X ✗

3 5 x 7 = ☐ ✓ X ✗

4 How many fours in sixteen? ☐ ✓ X ✗

5 How much is £10 and £18 and £12? ☐ ✓ X ✗

6 How many millimetres in two centimetres? ☐ ✓ X ✗

7 How many minutes in two hours? ☐ ✓ X ✗

8 You are playing cards and turn up a six, a three and a four; your sister turns up a seven, a four and a five. Who wins, and by how much? ☐ ✓ X ✗

9 If the minute hand of a clock goes half-way round the dial, how many minutes is that? ☐ ✓ X ✗

10 If you save £1 a week, how long will it take you to save £18? ☐ ✓ X ✗

11 If a car is travelling at 60 kilometres per hour (k.p.h.) how far will it travel in one and a half hours? ☐ ✓ X ✗

12 If you and your two friends have £1.20 between you and you both have the same amount, how much do you have each? ☐ ✓ X ✗

13 In your stamp collection you only need 15 more stamps to have 100 different French stamps. How many French stamps do you have at the moment? ☐ ✓ X ✗

14 You have fifty marbles. Your brother has ten fewer marbles than you, and your sister has ten fewer than your brother. How many marbles does your sister have? ☐ ✓ X ✗

15 A snail moves 10 centimetres in 10 minutes. How long will it take to cover a metre? ☐ ✓ X ✗

Always check your answers

☐ score

15

Working out on the back of your hand is not allowed

3B

1 Add 3 and 4 and 5.

2 Take 7 away from 12.

3 9 x 3 =

4 How many eights in forty?

5 How much is £7 and £8 and £15?

6 How many centimetres in two metres?

7 How many minutes in an hour and a quarter?

8 You roll a pair of dice. The first time you get a six and a two, the next time a five and a four. What is the difference?

9 If the minute hand of a clock goes one and a half times round the dial, how many minutes is that?

10 You have put 50p a week in your money box, and now you have saved £7.50. How many weeks have you been saving?

11 If the driver of a car travelling at 60 k.p.h. stops for a ten-minute break every hour, how far does he travel in two hours?

12 Your uncle leaves £10 to be divided equally between you and your three brothers. How much do you get?

13 You have 35 CDs, your friend has 17 more than you. How many does he have?

14 You start with 60 sweets. You eat half on the first day and then eat half of the remainder on the second day. How many do you have left?

15 The sea is washing away a cliff at the rate of 3 metres a year. The front of a holiday bungalow is 12 metres from the cliff edge. In how many years will the front door be at the cliff edge?

Think before you write!

score

15

12

When in doubt – guess!

3C

GUESS!

1 Add all the numbers from 1 to 10. 55. ✓ ✗ ✗

2 Take 9 away from 18. 9. ✓ ✗ ✗

3 11 x 4 = 44 ✓ ✗ ✗

4 How many threes in thirty-three? 11. ✓ ✗ ✗

5 How much is £12 and £10 and £18? £40 ✓ ✗ ✗

6 How many metres in two kilometres? 2000 ✓ ✗ ✗

7 How many minutes in two and a half hours? 150 ✓ ✗ ✗

8 Playing on a machine at the funfair you win £1, lose 50p and then win £1.50. How much do you end up with? £2·00 ✓ ✗ ✗

  ✓ ✗ ✗

9 If the hour hand of a clock goes half-way round the dial, how much time has gone by? 6 hrs ✓ ✗ ✗

10 If you save £1 a week, how much sooner will you save £20 than if you saved 50p a week? 9×9 8. ✓ ✗ ✗

✗ 11 If you can cycle at 20 k.p.h., how long does it take you to cycle one kilometre? ✓ ✗ ✗

ans: 2'

12 You win £25 in an essay competition and you give half of it to your sister. How much do you give her? ✓ ✗ ✗

13 You can throw a tennis ball 30 metres; your friend can throw it 3 metres less than you. How far can he throw it? ✓ ✗ ✗

14 Your brother has 10p more than you, your sister 10p less than you. If your sister has 20p, how much does your brother have? ✓ ✗ ✗

15 A hare can run at 45 k.p.h. If it runs for 20 minutes and then lies down and goes to sleep, how far will it have gone? ✓ ✗ ✗

Only the answers go in the boxes score

15

13

The check test is an oral test

3D Check Test

The adult asks the questions, the child gives the answers.
Any mistakes should be followed up.

1 Add all the numbers from 1 to 10.

2 Take 7 away from 12.

3 9 x 3 =

4 How many fours in sixteen?

5 How many threes in thirty-three?

6 How many millimetres in two centimetres?

7 How many minutes in an hour and a quarter?

8 You are playing cards and turn up a six, a three and a four; your sister turns up a seven, a four and a five. Who wins, and by how much?

9 If the hour hand of a clock goes half-way round the dial, how much time has gone by?

10 If you save £1 a week, how much sooner will you save £20 than if you saved 50p a week?

11 If the driver of a car travelling at 60 k.p.h. stops for a ten-minute break every hour, how far does he travel in two hours?

12 You win £25 in an essay competition and you give half of it to your sister. How much do you give her?

13 You have 35 CDs, your friend has 17 more than you. How many does he have?

14 You have fifty marbles, your brother has ten fewer than you, and your sister has ten fewer than your brother. How many marbles does your sister have?

15 A hare can run at 45 k.p.h. If it runs for 20 minutes and then lies down and goes to sleep, how far will it have gone?

No pencil needed for the check test

Concentrate!

4A

1 Add 17 and 6.

2 Take 8 away from 15.

3 5 x 8 =

4 How many sixes in eighteen?

5 How much is 65p and 45p?

6 How many metres in half a kilometre?

7 If you leave home at eight o'clock and arrive at school at quarter to nine, how long has it taken you?

8 A darts player scores 2, 16 and 14 with three darts. What is his total score?

9 You go to sleep at nine o'clock every night and wake up at seven in the morning. How long are you asleep?

10 For your holiday you save £5 a month for six months. How much do you save?

11 If you can do 100 skips in 3 minutes, how long does it take you to do 50 skips?

12 You have seen two purple cars today, yesterday you saw twice as many. How many purple cars have you seen in the two days?

13 When you look in your box of marbles you find 15 marbles, 8 fewer than you expected. How many did you expect to find?

14 Today you scored 18 out of 20 in a spelling test, 5 more than yesterday. How many did you score yesterday?

15 You measure your thumb-nail and it is $1\frac{1}{2}$ centimetres long. How many millimetres is that?

You'd be lost without a brain!

score

15

Better a nearly-right answer than no answer at all

4B

1 Add 18 and 9.   ☐ ✓ ✗ ✗

2 Take 9 away from 21.   ☐ ✓ ✗ ✗

3 5 x 6 =   ☐ ✓ ✗ ✗

4 How many threes in twenty-one?   ☐ ✓ ✗ ✗

5 How much is £14, £7 and £2?   ☐ ✓ ✗ ✗

6 How many centimetres in half a metre?   ☐ ✓ ✗ ✗

7 If the train leaves your local station at a quarter past two and reaches London two hours later, at what time does it arrive?   ☐ ✓ ✗ ✗

8 On a computer game you score two twenties and a fifteen. What is your total score?   ☐ ✓ ✗ ✗

9 If you go to bed every night at the same time and sleep ten hours, how many hours are you awake during the day?   ☐ ✓ ✗ ✗

10 If it is 500 metres round the race track, how many times do you go round for 1 kilometre?   ☐ ✓ ✗ ✗

11 You have found twenty conkers, four times as many as last week. How many did you find last week?   ☐ ✓ ✗ ✗

12 There are twenty pears on your tree this year, twelve fewer than last year. How many were there last year?   ☐ ✓ ✗ ✗

13 Your bus fare cost you £2.25, 50p more than you expected. How much did you expect it would cost?   ☐ ✓ ✗ ✗

14 If you are $1\frac{1}{2}$ metres tall, how many centimetres is that?   ☐ ✓ ✗ ✗

15 If a cake is cut into quarters and then each quarter is cut in half, how many pieces is that?   ☐ ✓ ✗ ✗

☐ score

The check-list makes sure you know it

15

16

Practice makes you quicker

4C

1 Add 21 and 11.

2 Take 12 away from 27.

3 9 x 2 =

4 How many fives in forty?

5 How much is £7, £8 and £15?

6 How many millimetres in half a centimetre?

7 At the beginning of the year there were 32 children in your class. Later on, 5 left, but 3 new children have come in. How many children are there in the class now?

8 Playing cricket you score a four in each of three overs, and then a six in the fourth over before being caught out. How many did you score altogether?

9 Your mother can get to work in 15 minutes in the morning, but coming home in the rush hour takes three times as long. How long does the return journey take?

10 If a car is going at 60 kilometres an hour, how far does it go in one minute?

11 Your weekly pocket money is £1.50, three times as much as last year. How much was it last year?

12 If a square room has walls each three metres long, how far is it all the way round the room?

13 If your school starts at nine o'clock and finishes at four o'clock, how many hours are you at school if you don't go home to lunch?

14 If a car's petrol tank holds seventy litres and it is half full, how much petrol is there in the tank?

15 Your grandfather gives you £10 for your savings account, doubling the amount you have in it. How much did you have before?

score

15

Simple sums are best done in your head

The check test is an oral test

4D Check Test

The adult asks the questions, the child gives the answers.
Any mistakes should be followed up.

1 Add 21 and 11.

2 Take 9 away from 21.

3 5 x 6 =

4 How many sixes in eighteen?

5 How much is £7, £8 and £15?

6 How many metres in half a kilometre?

7 If the train leaves your local station at a quarter past two and reaches London two hours later, at what time does it arrive?

8 A darts player scores 2, 16 and 14 with three darts.
What is his total score?

9 Your mother can get to work in 15 minutes in the morning, but coming home in the rush hour takes three times as long. How long does the return journey take?

10 For your holiday you save £5 a month for six months. How much do you save?

11 You have found twenty conkers, four times as many as last week. How many did you find last week?

12 If a square room has walls each three metres long, how far is it all the way round the room?

13 Your bus fare cost you £2.25, 50p more than you expected. How much did you expect it would cost?

14 Today you scored 18 out of 20 in a spelling test, 5 more than yesterday. How many did you score yesterday?

15 Your grandfather gives you £10 for your savings account, doubling the amount you have in it. How much did you have before?

No pencil needed for the check test

Remember – you won't always have a calculator handy!

5A

1 Add 27 and 18.

2 Take 17 away from 32.

3 6 x 9 =

4 How many sixes in forty-eight?

5 How much is £1.25 and £1.27?

6 How many millimetres in 2¹/₂ centimetres?

7 If you start with 20 marbles, lose 9 and then win 12, how many do you end up with?

8 If there are ten one-litre lemonade bottles but half of them are only half full, how many litres are left to drink?

9 When your father pays for the groceries at the supermarket check-out, he gets £1.73 change from a £10 note. How much did the groceries cost?

10 If a kilogramme of biscuits is divided equally into two bags, how many grammes are there in each bag?

11 You are 1 metre 53 cm tall, 13 cm taller than your brother. How tall is he?

12 Your mother puts a pie in the oven at half past five. If it takes an hour and a quarter to cook, at what time will it be ready?

13 Your white mouse is in a square cage, each side of which is 50 cm long. If he runs all the way round the edge just once, how far does he run?

14 You have 50 g of small sweets and you have to make up paper bags of 5 g each. How many bags of sweets will there be?

15 If ³/₄ kg of biscuits costs £1.50 how much will a kilogramme cost?

Learn to do it in your head!

score

15

19

If you want a rough guess round up or down to the nearest 10

5B

1 Add 19 and 31. ⌴ ✓ ✗ ✗

2 Take 19 away from 31. ⌴ ✓ ✗ ✗

3 7 x 8 = ⌴ ✓ ✗ ✗

4 How many eights in fifty-six? ⌴ ✓ ✗ ✗

5 How much is £1.07 and £2.35? ⌴ ✓ ✗ ✗

6 How many metres in 2¹/₂ kilometres? ⌴ ✓ ✗ ✗

7 Take 20 paces forwards, 2 backwards and then 13 paces forwards. How many paces forward are you from where you started? ⌴ ✓ ✗ ✗

8 If a car does ten kilometres to a litre of petrol, how many litres has it used up in 30 kilometres? ⌴ ✓ ✗ ✗

9 Your father buys butter at 82p, sugar at 68p and eggs at 73p. Round up or down to the nearest 10p. What is the total cost worked out in this way? ⌴ ✓ ✗ ✗

10 If 8 children (a ¹/₄ of the class) are off sick, how many children are there in the class usually? ⌴ ✓ ✗ ✗

11 You are half-way to school when you realize that you will be late if you don't run. You run twice as fast as you walk and you get there in five minutes. How long does it take you to do the *whole* journey *walking*? ⌴ ✓ ✗ ✗

12 You get ¹⁶/₂₀ for a spelling test. Your friend gets only three-quarters as many marks as you. How many does *he* get out of twenty? ⌴ ✓ ✗ ✗

13 If cooking apples weigh 100 g each, how many would you get in a kilogramme? ⌴ ✓ ✗ ✗

14 If your sister gets £4 a week pocket money, you get half of that, and your brother gets half as much as you – how much does he get? ⌴ ✓ ✗ ✗

15 If a train leaving at three o'clock is a quarter of an hour late on a journey that should take only an hour, at what time does it arrive? ⌴ ✓ ✗ ✗

How to round up or down to the nearest 10p:
50p, 51p, 52p, 53p, 54p all become 50p.
55p, 56p, 57p, 58p, 59p all become 60p, and so on.
Remember 5 rounds upwards.

⌴ score

| 15 |

The brain – man's first computer

5C

1 Add 27 and 25.

2 Take 27 away from 45.

3 10 x 9 =

4 How many elevens in seventy-seven?

5 How much is £3.70 and £1.35?

6 How many centimetres in 3½ metres?

7 If you start with £5, spend 60p on sweets, 40p on a comic, and then earn 50p for running an errand, how much do you end up with?

8 If a bus leaves at 13.00 hours on the 24-hour clock and arrives half an hour later, what is the time of arrival on the 12-hour clock?

9 You weigh 25 kilos, 500 grammes more than you did six months ago. How much did you weigh then?

10 If a car is travelling at 60 km an hour, how far does it travel in 30 seconds?

11 If a cake is cut into quarters, and then each piece is cut into quarters again, how many pieces are there?

12 There are three trees: one is 31 metres tall, one is 21 metres tall. The height of the third one is half-way between the other two. How tall is it?

13 David has 20 marbles, Andrew has twice as many but Richard has only a quarter of what Andrew has. How many marbles has Richard got?

14 If your little sister's bricks are 10 centimetres high, how many will she need to build a tower 1½ metres high?

15 If you buy two chocolate bars at 35p each, how much change will you have from £1?

Learn how to program your brain!

score

15

The check test is an oral test

5D Check Test

The adult asks the questions, the child gives the answers.
Any mistakes should be followed up.

1 Add 27 and 25.

2 Take 19 away from 31.

3 7 x 8 =

4 How many sixes in forty-eight?

5 How much is £3.70 and £1.35?

6 How many millimetres in 2$\frac{1}{2}$ centimetres?

7 Take 20 paces forwards, 2 backwards and then 13 paces forwards. How many paces forward are you from where you started?

8 If there are ten one-litre lemonade bottles but half of them are only half full, how many litres are left to drink?

9 You weigh 25 kilos, 500 grammes more than you did six months ago How much did you weigh then?

10 If a kilogramme of biscuits is divided equally into two bags, how many grammes are there in each bag?

11 You are half-way to school when you realize that you will be late if you don't run. You run twice as fast as you walk and you get there in five minutes. How long does it take you to do the *whole* journey *walking*?

12 There are three trees: one is 31 metres tall, one is 21 metres tall. The height of the third one is half-way between the other two. How tall is it?

13 If cooking apples weigh 100 g each, how many would you get in a kilogramme?

14 You have 50 g of small sweets and you have to make up paper bags of 5 g each. How many bags of sweets will there be?

15 If you buy two chocolate bars at 35p each, how much change will you have from £1?

No pencil needed for the check test

22

Always look for a short cut

6A

1 Add 17 and 15 and 13.

2 Add 15 and 35 and then take away 12.

3 3 x 3 x 3 =

4 How many nines in eighty-one?

5 Take 80p away from £2.00.

6 Add 1½ metres and 50 centimetres.

7 What is a third of 90?

8 How long is one side of a square metre?

9 These numbers make a pattern. What would the next number be? 12, 20, 28, 36, ...

10 Two cars set out at the same time to a town 80 kilometres away. One car travels at 80 kilometres per hour, the other at 40 kilometres per hour. How much longer does the slower car take?

11 What is 10% of £100?

12 A leather football costs £40. A good plastic one costs half as much and the cheapest one costs a *quarter of that*. How much is the cheapest one?

13 You are going to see a film which starts at 7 pm and finishes at 9.30 pm. What are the times of starting and finishing on the 24-hour clock?

14 If you were born on the 21st January 1985, how old would you be on the 18th June 1995 in years and completed months?

15 If your parents buy six 3-metre floorboards at £4 a metre, how much do they cost?

Use your brain to save your brain

score

15

23

There may be an easy way and a hard way. Think …

6B

1 Add 19 and 12 and 30.

2 Add 30 and 15 and then take away 14.

3 4 x 4 x 2 =

4 How many twelves in seventy-two?

5 Take 75p away from £2.50.

6 Add 3$\frac{1}{2}$ centimetres and 5 millimetres.

7 What is a quarter of 120?

8 How long is one side of a square kilometre?

9 In a supermarket you buy a tin of beans at 47p, a packet of bacon at £1.23 and a packet of tea-bags at 93p. Rounding up or down to the nearest 10p, what is the 'guess' price altogether?

10 On your new bicycle you can travel at 30 kilometres per hour. How long does it take you to get to your school 3 kilometres away?

11 What is 10% of £10?

12 These numbers make a pattern. What would the next number be?
601, 701, 801, 901, ...

13 Your father says he will pay you 20p for every bag of grass cuttings you collect, and 10p bonus for every six bags. You fill 18 bags. How much do you earn?

14 If the 20th September is a Monday, what day of the week will 4th October be?

15 A 1 kg box of cornflakes costs £1.80. A 500 g box costs £1.05. How much do you save in the long term by buying the kilo box?

Rounding makes it easier to add up several small amounts with near-miss accuracy

score

15

Using your brain makes life easier

6C

1 Add 38 and 18 and 33. ☐ ✓ X ✕

2 Add 17 and 47 and then halve the total. ☐ ✓ X ✕

3 2 x 10 x 4 = ☐ ✓ X ✕

4 How many twelves in one hundred and twenty? ☐ ✓ X ✕

5 Take £1.28 away from £4.33. ☐ ✓ X ✕

6 If three boys are 1 m 50 cm, 1 m 60cm and
1 m 70 cm tall, what is their average height? ☐ ✓ X ✕

7 What is a third of 180? ☐ ✓ X ✕

8 If a table is 1 metre long and 2 metres wide,
how far is it round the edge (the *perimeter*)? ☐ ✓ X ✕

9 Your mother hires a rowing boat to go on the
lake in the public park. It costs £4 for the first
hour then 50p for each 10 minutes after that.
You return the boat after 1¹/₂ hours. How much
does it cost your mother? ☐ ✓ X ✕

10 In a litre bottle of cola there is only 125 ml
(millilitres) left. How much has been drunk
(in millilitres)? ☐ ✓ X ✕

11 What is one quarter expressed as a decimal? ☐ ✓ X ✕

12 Your father wants to tile the top of a coffee
table measuring 40 cm by 80 cm. The tiles are
10cm square. How many will he need? ☐ ✓ X ✕

13 These numbers make a pattern. What would
the next number be? 14, 18, 22, 26, ... ☐ ✓ X ✕

= 14

14 A kilo of biscuits costs only £2.40 because you
get 250 g free. What would it cost to buy just
250 g of biscuits at the normal price? ☐ ✓ X ✕

15 You have saved up to buy a mountain bike which
cost £200 when you first saw it. But the price has
increased by 10%. How much does it cost now? ☐ ✓ X ✕

☐ score

There is no substitute for your brain

15

The check test is an oral test

6D Check Test

The adult asks the questions, the child gives the answers.
Any mistakes should be followed up.

1 Add 38 and 18 and 33.

2 Add 30 and 15 and then take away 14.

3 4 x 4 x 2 =

4 How many nines in eighty-one?

5 Take £1.28 away from £4.33.

6 Add 1^1/$_2$ metres and 50 centimetres.

7 What is a quarter of 120?

8 How long is one side of a square metre?

9 Your mother hires a rowing boat to go on the lake in the public park. It costs £4 for the first hour then 50p for each 10 minutes after that. You return the boat after 1^1/$_2$ hours. How much does it cost your mother?

10 Two cars set out at the same time to a town 80 kilometres away. One car travels at 80 kilometres per hour, the other at 40 kilometres per hour. How much longer does the slower car take?

11 What is 10% of £10?

12 Your father wants to tile the top of a coffee table measuring 40 cm by 80 cm. The tiles are 10 cm square. How many will he need?

13 Your father says he will pay you 20p for every bag of grass cuttings you collect, and 10p bonus for every six bags. You fill 18 bags. How much do you earn?

14 If you were born on the 21st January 1985, how old would you be on the 18th June 1995 in years and completed months?

15 You have saved up to buy a mountain bike which cost £200 when you first saw it. But the price has increased by 10%. How much does it cost now?

No pencil needed for the check test

26

Can you think for yourself?

7A

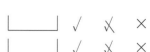

1 Add 36 and 42 and 52. ☐ ✓ ✗ ✗

2 Add 36 and 36 and divide by 9. ☐ ✓ ✗ ✗

3 (3 x 6) + (3 x 7) = ☐ ✓ ✗ ✗

4 How many tens in two hundred and ten? ☐ ✓ ✗ ✗

5 Take £1.67 from £3.50. ☐ ✓ ✗ ✗

6 At an auction four bikes are sold at £40 each and four at £45 each. What was the average price? ☐ ✓ ✗ ✗

7 Your cat eats four 50p tins of cat meat a week. How much does it cost to feed him for a year? ☐ ✓ ✗ ✗

8 What is the perimeter of a rectangular field 50 metres wide and 100 metres long? ☐ ✓ ✗ ✗

9 How many days are there in 100 years, ignoring leap years? ☐ ✓ ✗ ✗

10 In the summer you catch the Hovercraft from Dover to Calais, leaving at 13.00 hours. The journey takes 40 minutes, but French Summer Time is an hour ahead of British Summer Time. At what time do you arrive (on the 24-hour clock) by *French* Summer Time? ☐ ✓ ✗ ✗

11 What is one-third expressed as a decimal? ☐ ✓ ✗ ✗

12 Your parents buy a second-hand car for £4,000. They pay a 25% deposit. The rest of the money they borrow from the bank repaying over the year. The bank adds a flat 10% interest charge to the amount they borrow. How much does the car cost your parents, including the interest? ☐ ✓ ✗ ✗

13 If a square piece of paper has an area of 16 square centimetres (16 cm^2), how long are the sides? ☐ ✓ ✗ ✗

14 These numbers make a pattern. What will the next number be? 130, 110, 90, 70 .... ☐ ✓ ✗ ✗

15 Your mother wants to buy a fitted carpet for the sitting room to cover all of the floor. The room is 4 m by 6 m. How many square metres of carpet will she need to buy? ☐ ✓ ✗ ✗

Your brain – the only computer that will last seventy years

☐ score

| 15 |

You won't always have a calculator, but you're never without your head

7B

1 Add 51 and 23 and 38.

2 Add 45 and 39 and divide by 7.

3 (4 x 8) + (9 x 5) =

4 How many nines in nine hundred and nine?

5 Take £3.82 from £4.97.

6 The rainfall for one week is 13 mm on Sunday, nothing on Monday and Tuesday, 7 mm on Wednesday, 10 mm on Thursday, 1 mm on Friday and 4 mm on Saturday. What was the *average* in millimetres for the seven days?

7 What is three-quarters of forty-eight?

8 You have to cut 6 cm rods from a steel rod 50 cm in length. How many rods can you cut?

9 You take two books out from the library on the 17th July but don't return them until the 21st August. If you don't take them back after two weeks, you pay a fine of 20p for the first week and 30p a week after that. How much do you have to pay in fines?

10 If a football match lasts 45 minutes each way, with a 15-minute interval and 10 minutes extra for injuries that held up the game, how long did the game last from start to finish?

11 What is $1\frac{1}{2}$ expressed as a decimal?

12 You give 20p for a poppy on Remembrance Day; your father gives two and a half times as much. How much does he give?

13 If a square piece of paper has an area of 25 square centimetres, what are the lengths of the sides?

14 If firemen are pumping water from a 10,000-litre tank at the rate of 250 litres a minute, how long will the supply last?

15 These numbers make a pattern. What will the next number be? 36, 49, 64, 81 ....

Watch it! Some of these are easy to get right – and easy to get wrong!

28

score

15

If you've got this far, your brain's in better shape

7C

1 Add 72 and 15 and 28.

2 Add 62 and 59 and divide by 11.

3 (6 x 6) + (7 x 7) =

4 How many twenty-ones in a hundred and sixty-eight?

5 Take £7.34 from £9.09.

6 Your batting average for the last season was 32. This season you have scored 28, 63, 42 and 35. How much better is your average so far this season?

7 What is one-fifth of a hundred?

8 How many pieces 10 cm x 5 cm can you cut out of a piece of wood 1 metre long and 50 cm wide?

9 If you wind up an eight-day clock on the 1st January, how many times will you have had to wind it up by the 2nd March in a leap year?

10 If a 3-kilowatt electric fire costs 8p per hour per kilowatt, how much does it cost to run it for 30 minutes?

11 What is 8¾ expressed as a decimal?

12 If a rectangular room is 4 metres wide and 5 metres long, how many square metres of carpet will you need to cover half of the floor area?

13 These numbers make a pattern. What would the next number be?   1, 3, 6, 10 ....

14 A baby was born on September 22nd, seventeen days earlier than expected. What date was he expected to be born on?

15 Petrol costs 60p a litre and a car does 5 kilometres to the litre in town, 6 kilometres to the litre on the motorway. What is the difference in cost between doing a kilometre in town and doing a kilometre on the motorway?

Brains need exercise too!

score

15

29

The check test is an oral test

7D Check Test

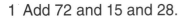

The adult asks the questions, the child gives the answers.
Any mistakes should be followed up.

1 Add 72 and 15 and 28.

2 Add 45 and 39 and divide by 7.

3 (4 x 8) + (9 x 5) =

4 How many tens in two hundred and ten?

5 Take £7.34 from £9.09.

6 At an auction four bikes are sold at £40 each and four at £45 each. What was the average price?

7 What is three-quarters of forty-eight?

8 What is the perimeter of a rectangular field 50 metres wide and 100 metres long?

9 If you wind up an eight-day clock on the 1st January, how many times will you have had to wind it up by the 2nd March in a leap year?

10 In the summer you catch the Hovercraft from Dover to Calais, leaving at 13.00 hours. The journey takes 40 minutes, but French Summer Time is an hour ahead of British Summer Time. At what time do you arrive (on the 24-hour clock) by *French* Summer Time?

11 What is $1\frac{1}{2}$ expressed as a decimal?

12 If a rectangular room is 4 metres wide and 5 metres long, how many square metres of carpet will you need to cover half of the floor area?

13 If a square piece of paper has an area of 25 square centimetres, what are the lengths of the sides?

14 These numbers make a pattern. What will the next number be?
130, 110, 90, 70 ....

15 Petrol costs 60p a litre and a car does 5 kilometres to the litre in town, 6 kilometres to the litre on the motorway. What is the difference in cost between doing a kilometre in town and doing a kilometre on the motorway?

No pencil needed for the check test

You do this on your own!

End-of-Book Test

1 Add 17 and 14.

2 Add 15 and 20 and 25.

3 Take 11 away from 30.

4 Add 28 and 14 and then take away 19.

5 7 x 6 =

6 How many eights in four hundred?

7 How many twenty-fives in two hundred and fifty?

8 What is 65p more than £1.90?

9 Take £2.37 away from £7.18.

10 How many millimetres in 17.5 centimetres?

11 Add $1\frac{1}{4}$ metres and 37 centimetres.

12 What is an eighth of 16?

13 What is a twenty-fifth of 125?

14 If an athlete wins the 5000-metre race in 25 minutes, what is her speed in kilometres per hour?

15 You buy a drawing book at 99p, a stencil at 75p and a pencil at 42p. Rounding up or down to the nearest 10p, what is your guess-estimate total cost?

16 What is $12\frac{1}{2}$% of £100?

17 Two cars set out for a town 100 kilometres away. The first car (A) travels at 60 k.p.h. The second car (B) leaves half an hour later but travels at 90 k.p.h. Which car gets there first – A or B?

18 The sports shop has a tennis racquet for £30, but the best one costs half as much again. How much is the best one?

19 You need £10 to buy a calculator, but you are 20% short. How much do you have?

20 What is 1.33 expressed as a fraction?

21 Your times for winning the 100 metres this term are 15 secs, 14 secs, 17 secs and 18 secs. What is your *average* time?

22 If you run twice round the perimeter of a rectangular field 70 m x 130 m, how far have

you run?

23 How many carpet squares 50 cm x 50 cm will be needed to cover a floor with an area of four square metres?

24 If you buy seventeen 10p balloons for a party, how much change will you have from £2?

25 If you scored $^{15}/_{15}$ on test 1A, two-thirds of that on test 4A and only half that on test 7A, what was your score on 7A?

| | ✓ | ✗ | ✗ |

How good are you at mental arithmetic?

	score
25	

How many stars?

	*	**	***
Age 9 or below	5 – 10	11 – 17	18 +
Age 10 – 11	7 – 12	13 – 19	20 +

ANSWERS

1A	1B	1C	1D	2A	2B	2C	2D
1. 7	1. 8	1. 15	1. 15	1. 13	1. 18	1. 12	1. 12
2. 6	2. 6	2. 5	2. 6	2. 9	2. 9	2. 5	2. 9
3. 15	3. 16	3. 25	3. 16	3. 24	3. 28	3. 16	3. 28
4. 4	4. 3	4. 5	4. 4	4. 3	4. 6	4. 12	4. 3
5. 100	5. 5	5. 12	5. 12	5. 10	5. 6	5. 22	5. 22
6. 7	6. £2.35	6. 90p	6. 7	6. £1.05	6. 90p	6. 90p	6. £1.05
7. 6	7. 13	7. 18	7. 13	7. 11	7. 14	7. 12 red	7. 14
8. 12	8. 9	8. 13	8. 12	8. 10	8. 19	10 blue	8. 10
9. 2	9. 18	9. £1.60	9. £1.60	9. 50p	9. 90p	8. 23	9. £1
10. £1.20	10. 10	10. 4	10. £1.20	10. 3	10. 18	9. £1	10. 3
11. 12	11. 8	11. 10	11. 8	11. 6	11. 8	10. 50 mins	11. 8
12. 0	12. 50p	12. £3	12. £3	12. 75p	12. 15	11. 12	12. £2.01
13. 22	13. 25p	13. 30p	13. 25p	13. 20p	13. 40p	12. £2.01	13. 40p
14. 3	14. 17	14. $^{1}/_{2}$	14. 3	14. $^{1}/_{4}$	14. 2	13. £1.50	14. $^{1}/_{4}$
15. £2	15. 4	15. 25p	15. 25p	15. 75p	15. $^{15}/_{20}$	14. 5	15. 30
						15. 30	